G000126285

Send me a parcel with a hundred lovely things

Send me a parcel with a hundred lovely things

By

Carry Gorney

First Printing: 2014

ISBN:
Paperback - 978-1-910667-01-9
mobi - 978-1-910667-02-6
epub - 978-1-910667-03-3

Cover Design by Spiffing Covers Ltd.

Ragged Clown Publishing
        c/o 1 Ferdinand Place, London, NW1 8EE

Contact: sendmeaparcel@raggedclown.co.uk

www.carrygorney.co.uk/sendmeaparcel

Ordering Information:
Special discounts are available on quantity purchases by corporations, associations, educators, and others. For details, contact the publisher at the above listed address.

U.S. trade bookstores and wholesalers:
Please contact
Jonathan Kelner: jk@kelnerconsulting.com

Illustrations and cover montage image by Carry Gorney

Photographic Archive includes images by:
Alex Levac
Ponch Hawkes
Tony Coult
Bob Chase
Roland Kemp
Maggie Gathercole
Peter Mount

I'm sorry if I have omitted anyone; please contact me and I will amend future editions

The author

Carry Gorney is a writer and artist, who worked previously in both the public and private sector as a systemic psychotherapist. She has a son, nephew and step-daughter. Carry, her partner, a caramel dog and a black and white cat split their time between London and Alsace.

Contents

Gornitzky/Weiss - Family Tree

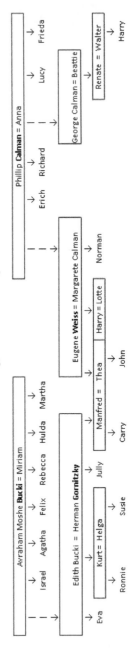

FOREWORD

Carry Gorney draws us into two worlds: the bright, warm, intense and comfortingly insular world of her German-Jewish family – refugees from Nazi Germany; and later into the developing counter-culture and community arts movement of the Sixties and Seventies – another colourful arena, but wider, more daring and innovative. She has taken us from safety and tradition, to adventure, exploration and innovation.

Set against the dreariness of post-war Leeds, with its subdued colours, boiled cabbage and smog, Gorney's childhood home life is vibrant, creative and almost luminous. At school she is made to knit in grey, but in her mother's knitting group the wool is rainbow coloured and fluffy, and the results jewelled, sequinned, bedecked in pom-poms and flowers. The group is celebratory and loving, a familiar safe haven for the displaced, and sustains the women throughout their new life in a comparatively dull and suspicious Britain.

From her parents' letters, Carry Gorney provides a unique insight into life in an internment camp on the Isle of Man, where her father was detained as an enemy alien. His frustration is palpable, and her mother's efforts to sustain him – with hope, the many letters and parcels - of mainly food - are almost superhuman. The family's cooking is as luscious as their knitting. There is a great physicality about Gorney's writing: the women with their ample backsides, corsets and chilblains, Grandma's perfume and the little wisps of hair on her neck. You can almost smell the warm, buttery, crumbly cakes and the fresh coffee, schmaltz, lamb's tongue. Evocative details crowd the memoir: photos with scalloped edges, the Clarks foot x-ray machine, one BBC channel, playing hopscotch, wafer-thin airmail paper, roll-ons and suspenders. But in the background are unsettling reminders of the war – her father's survivor's guilt and sudden rages, old photos of friends and relatives who have 'disappeared', a tinge of anti-Semitism in the background, along with the English resentment and suspicion of refugees.

From the almost claustrophobic atmosphere of her childhood and the stifling respectability of the Fifties, Gorney breaks free, and with enormous energy and wholehearted involvement, joins the counter-culture – a world of street theatre, activism, squatting, sexual freedom, collectives, women's liberation and consciousness-raising groups. But she brings her past with her - the vivid creativity of the women, her father's musicality and her own understanding of, and sympathy for, the displaced, alien and dispossessed. She seeks the outsiders to work with: teenagers on the edge, young children with fractured lives, refugee families, the poor and the mentally ill. We journey with her through the rise and fall of the community and radical arts movement, the advent of Thatcher and the National Curriculum and her own breakdown and recovery, helped again by knitting, another prop from the past, which brings her back to 'safe, female territory'. Through a roller-coaster journey, this book shows us the importance of community, history, culture, freedom and imagination.

Michele Hanson
London, 2014

PROLOGUE

The Egg

The girl is folded into darkness. Inside the egg, she listens, her hands in her lap.

"Once upon a time…" the explorer begins.

The children listen mesmerized by the giant turquoise egg in their midst.

"I climbed mountains and crossed valleys… "

They hear scratching. Some shrink back, others put their hands over their ears, one or two gasp, perhaps imagining the beating of wings or a beak pecking at the shell.

Inside the darkness the girl wears shimmering water coloured fabric. Long pointed sleeves are edged with multi-coloured braid, fine plaits hang from her cap. Her finger and toenails are painted silver.

The explorer recounts his journey, the turquoise egg strapped to his back, over many continents. He sailed across raging seas and galloped through icy wastelands on the backs of wild horses.

The children huddle together for warmth as he describes violent storms. They become the howling wind by blowing through their fingers and make the sound of raindrops by tapping on the side of the egg.

The girl inside listens to pitter-patter on her shell. She sways gently, hugging herself, and makes the egg tremble slightly. The sound of her humming mingles with the rain.

"Mister, there's someone in there."

"It's alive."

"It's singing now."

"Hey it's a girl singing."

"What's she saying?"

"Mister she might be scared."

Some grab the explorer's arm, or touch his face to make him notice.

He says nothing. He taps his hands twice, very softly, the children watch him carefully and as he fixes his attention on the egg, they turn too.

The girl listens, she waits, there's another tap, and another, two this time. A long pause, the next one is a little rhythm, one two three. She replies with the same rhythm and hears a gasp of excitement outside the egg. She smiles, leans forward as far as she can and waits for the next tentative rhythm to tap her reply. This conversation continues for a while. The children on the outside send increasingly complicated messages. The girl inside responds carefully, copying each rhythm as she hears it and adding a little message of her own in reply. No words are spoken.

She pushes her splayed fingers through the side of the egg; the children are excited.

"Mister, it's coming out, mister is it safe? Will it eat us?"

She pushes her hand through the shell and reaches out. Her face appears. She stares at them; they stare back, unsure whether to be thrilled or terrified. No one speaks.

She steps out of the egg and blinks, slowly getting used to the bright room. One or two take a step backwards. A little boy touches her shoulder blade gently. Maybe she has wings, she's a bird, or an angel.

"My name's Wayne" he says. She looks at him. "Wayne," she repeats in a whisper.

He turns to the explorer. "She can't be a bird, mister, she's no feathers. She said my name." He was jabbing at his own chest and jumping up and down.

"Name," repeats the girl, jabbing at her chest too.

"No, no, that's my name."

"What's yours?" asks a big girl at the front, putting her face close in case the stranger can't hear.

"Yours," the girl repeats, they touch each other's faces slowly.

"I'm not scared," a voice at the back of the room pipes up. A small girl with a mass of blonde curls steps forward bravely. "She can't hurt us, I bet she's scared."

"She could, she's bigger than us," says another voice.

"Nah, she's afraid, 'cos she's a stranger. We all know each other." The children were deciding that the girl was a stranger and was afraid.

"Tell us your name," says brave blonde curls, tugging at her arm. Will you be my friend?"

"Friend," repeats the stranger.

"We'll give you a name," says the boy at the back.

"My dog's called Spot, let's call her Spot."

"No, she ain't a dog"

"Mister, can we call her Barbie, like my doll?"

"Don't be daft, she ain't no Barbie."

"I know," says the boy with spectacles who'd been watching for a while, "I know, let's call her Zero"

"Why Zero?"

"Cos she doesn't know anything"

"We'll teach her," says the blonde curls.

"Zero" says spectacles, slowly holding the girl's hand, "Zero," he repeats pointing at her.

She's puzzled.

"You Zero," another child holds her hand gently.

The girl points at herself, "You Zero," she says and looks at Spectacles hopefully.

"Nearly," he says, "nearly, that's your name, what you're called, it's special."

"It's the beginning," says the big girl, watching carefully, sucking her thumb. "It's your beginning".

"Zero, it's your name, my mum says your name's the beginning of everything"

The explorer reminds the children how far away from home Zero has travelled inside an egg. He kept her safe, until she was ready to emerge.

To survive in a strange land, Zero needed her new friends. They understand this and overcome their own fears and suspicions. They make a place for her in their world. The children became teachers, the adult, became the child.

Emerging from an egg we might spread our wings and reach the sky. The watery costume reminds us that our ancestors might have emerged from the sea, with webbed feet. Wearing history in the sleeves, Zero stands outside our everyday like a Greek chorus or a Fool, coming from another time and if we speak a different language we come from another place.

This was a play performed with children with special needs; they understood about being outsiders. They took charge of Zero's entry into the world and eventually made a decision to release her into the wild, the wild of Milton Keynes.

In the beginning was the egg.

This is the story of a girl who chooses to step out of the egg into her memoir.

PART ONE

In the twilight of the vanishing world

...a story is not like a road to follow...it's more like a house. You go inside and stay there for a while, wondering back and forth and settling where you like and discovering how the room and corridors relate to each other, how the world outside is altered by being viewed from these windows.......
Alice Munro Selected Stories, 1968-1994

Chapter 1

2010

My mother is in hospital. She stirs from her deepening sleep. The nurse asks if she would like to see a rabbi.

"What would I want with a rabbi?" comes her sharp reply. She sleeps, I knit. I draw the curtains. She sleeps on. I turn my knitting.

The nurse enters carrying a blue folder. She turns to me with a brisk smile, points to the label, *End of Life Process*.

"I think we're here now." Mum's eyes open. The nurse explains to both of us that she needs to check out a few things;

"Your name?"

"Thea."

"How do you spell it?"

"*T- H-E-A*."

"Is that an English name? It's very unusual, I've heard of Theo for a boy."

"Theo, a boy." Thea whispers.

She's finding difficulty in moving her lips; they're very dry and cracked. The nurse dampens her mouth with a cotton swab soaked in glycerine.

Pause. The nurse tries again. "So, you are English?"

"Of course I'm bloody English. I was born and bred in Yorkshire, I'm Yorkshire."

"But you *are* Jewish?"

"Yes, of course." My mum closes her eyes to indicate the end of the conversation.

There's a pause. The nurse turns to me. "Shouldn't I call the rabbi?"

I watch my Mum travelling away from me in her sleep.

"There are many ways of being Jewish," I answer, "and hers has never involved a rabbi."

"I need to check her place of birth."

"Dewsbury."

Dewsbury, where the Jews come from, I used to think when I was little.

1976

In his dream, Manfred skips and jumps as he crosses the town square holding on to his grandfather's hand. The old man's long black coat is flapping open as he hurries along. He reaches up whenever a gust of wind threatens to blow away his wide-brimmed hat. Then he quickly clutches the child's hand again or grasps his shoulder. A freshly-slaughtered boiling fowl is in his other hand ready to be plucked and cooked for the Shabbos meal.

The little boy and his grandfather are humming the melodies for the Shabbos evening service; they hold hands and swing their arms to the rhythm. Avraham Moishe Bucki will lead the singing. He is the local rabbi. He will allow Manfred to attend if he behaves, even though it's past his bedtime.

I am standing, the remnants of clown make-up on my face, at the end of my father's hospital bed, hoping his eyes will open once more. I am clutching my backpack and am trying to catch his words... he whispers...*always keep the music in your life...*

2010

My mum had wanted to stay at home, well, in her London flat. Real home had been her bungalow in Leeds with the magnolia tree in the front garden; or perhaps her true home had been the top floor Berlin flat with a balcony where she and her friend did their homework and my granny brought them milk and cakes, all in a different language. As she became very old we sold her bungalow and she moved to our street in London. On removal day she watched me throw out packets of food, five years past their sell-by date. She watched me place her 1940s ironing board with the rubbish, her brown sofa carried out to the dump, her plates and dishes wrapped in newspaper. She couldn't remember the smiling friends on the faded dog-eared photographs as she threw them on to the bonfire.

I cried as I said goodbye to her magnolia tree, the dog whined, but she just turned her head away.

London. We were all exhausted. Her wall units had been assembled by midnight, but the next morning she wanted them down and remounted on the other wall. I took the wrong bag of clothes into Oxfam and chased back up the M1 to change them. She thought the Muslim neighbours who brought us food at the end of Ramadan were being friendly "because we're Jewish."

I trapped her dog's head in the gate whilst carrying her boxes into the flat. Lucky stood looking at me mournfully as I struggled to release her; I knelt down hugging her. "Sorry, sorry," I kept repeating, weeping again at this uprooting, at the overwhelming responsibility for my mother and her old dog.

1976

I visit my father in Leeds Infirmary. He's telling me about his life in Berlin, before the war. I use a cassette recorder to catch his tales.

We eat our fish and chips out of the Yorkshire Post newspaper and I hope to snuggle down into images from a pre-war Ashkenazi world, the beginning of the century before last.

The nuggets of his life are tucked into music. He slips away from his own story starting with words to describe a symphony, play a tune on the piano, find a 78rpm record. He makes me sit still. My father's stories go round in circles; they are stories within stories.

I'm suddenly listening to a crackly recording of Fritz Kreisler that my father carried in his only suitcase out of Berlin when he fled 40 years earlier. Now I don't know where I am, we are both flying over Europe like a Marc Chagall painting – except my image is of my father playing his accordion, not a goat playing a violin. My hand reaches out to a vanished world, a ragged clown, beneath a diamond sky.

2010

My mum was becoming frailer. My attempts in persuading her to have more care in the home were futile.

"Too expensive," she grumbled, "I'm OK I can manage."

She couldn't manage.

She was entitled to free palliative care; it was hard to make her understand that. She continued to live her life with the make do and mend mentality from World War Two; as though everything was still rationed and she must save every penny. Eventually, to please me, she agreed to be assessed. The neat lady from Social Services arrived.

"Very pleasant", mum conceded afterwards. She had perched on the edge of the sofa, eyeing two dozing dogs. She held a clipboard and apparently kept ticking boxes. Everything had gone well. Mobility aids could be brought into the house – yes, seemed a good idea especially if she didn't have to pay. Help getting in and out of the bath – yes, worth a try (she longed for a soak in warm scented water). Help with shopping - she didn't need, she had her family. Help with cooking - didn't need, she had us.

I should have been there; supporting her to maintain her independence meant we were rapidly losing ours. Her answers were more and more clipped; she was unable to face her increasing limitations. The nice lady with her clipboard resting on knees clamped together had leaned forward.

"Could you tell me about your finances, Mrs. G?"

"Finances," a sharp look, "what do you mean?" she asked glaring through thick-lensed spectacles.

"Uh-um, I'd like to know your pensions, your savings, whether you pay rent, you know just to decide what level of support we can offer...."

"What makes you think I'd tell you any of my secrets? It's not your business, these are my private affairs." She was getting increasingly agitated, even in the telling of this story. "It's my business, there's no law saying I have to tell you this... next you'll be asking for papers," she was almost shrieking now. "Papers, yes to prove who I am, to prove that I have a right to be here, this is my country I belong here, this is my home, I was even born here, and I don't want any foreigners coming through my door..."

The lady had stood up and was backing towards the door; my mum was pushing her out.

"You mind your own business, I won't have the state poking into my affairs, I won't. I don't need your help. I'm alright on my own."

That was it. I could find no way to re-open the discussion. We had to struggle on alone without help from the state.

1976

> *There is only one place for the enemy alien while the*
> *war lasts. That place is behind barbed wire.*
> Lieutenant Governor, Isle of Man, 1940

"Daddy, when did you learn to speak English?"

"I was proud to become an Englishman, I felt safe with the English bobby on his beat."

"But when could you say things in English?"

"You don't need the words to share your music."

"When could you understand, you know, people in shops?"

"It just came."

"Wasn't it embarrassing, not being able to speak? Did you go to evening classes?"

"When I was an enemy alien, in the internment camp they suggested we learnt to speak English properly – they wanted us to obliterate any trace of German, even the accent," he smiled at the impossibility of this. "The other inmates, older than me, wanted us to study English, classics, philosophy and science, everything you could imagine. Well, I already spoke English, not very well, but fluently enough. I hadn't the patience, you know. I was 26. I just was desperate to get out and get on with my life. One of the British officers asked me to help translating letters in the office. I hoped it would help me get my release through quickly, but anyway I liked working for the British, after all, as soon as the war ended, after naturalisation I would be British."

He now carefully places the stylus on another vinyl record, a Mozart symphony. I sit next to him and we follow the score together, as we had done since I was little. I sat on his knee listening to the Hallé orchestra in Leeds town hall on a Saturday night watching my father's finger travelling across the lines covered with black dots. Like Hebrew, it had been another language to decipher.

He falls asleep, but I still sit with my finger on the page, crochets, quavers and semi-quavers dancing before my eyes.

He often described how he carried his wicker chair in a procession of hundreds of men, prisoners like him, to the square in the middle of Hutchinson camp. They were going to listen to the concerts given by the Amadeus quartet, the pianists Rawicz and Landauer and even once, Richard Tauber.

He opens his eyes. "That's where I learned to read music."
"Where?"
At the Sefton Hotel, in Douglas."
"The Isle of Man? You said you were a prisoner there, what were you doing in a hotel?"
"There was a row of boarding houses along the seafront, enclosed by barbed wire and that was our prison. I was in the Sefton, on the top floor."

Room with a sea view! He always needed to see the sea on holiday.

"Frische Luft", *fresh air*, he would shout opening the windows. "Look baby, freedom." He'd point at the horizon. "We could sail anywhere." I'd stand on tiptoe, curious to see what freedom looked like; I could just see clouds scudding across a clear blue sky. I heard the waves; I tasted salt on my lips. I had no idea why it meant freedom.

"Yes, my room faced east. I used to get up early and watch the sun rise over the sea through the barbed wire. I'd imagine German boats appearing on the horizon, sailing towards us."

He turned to me. "I was frightened they would invade the island and find us Jews behind barbed wire like animals in cages."

Our eyes met, I understood. Freedom was a clear horizon, no boats

2010

My mum's favourite plants were wild strawberries. Her Aunty Frieda had taken her to the Grunewald suburb of Berlin, searching for tiny crimson berries nestling in the dappled shadows cast by tall conifers and birch trees. For many years she grew these timid plants under the apple tree in her Leeds garden.

Each harvest yielded no more than ten strawberries at a time. She saved them for my visits during the growing season, offering them in a glass bowl, a puddle of syrup at the bottom, topped with a miniature dollop of cream.

During her last months we used plastic grow-bags to plant the wild strawberries in her London back yard. She struggled outside, to pick them with gnarled fingers, stained yellow with nicotine. She sugared them and handed them to me in the same glass bowl when I came by after work.

1976

"Tell me about the music when you were on the Isle of Man."

"There was a piano in the lobby where we used to drink coffee. I'd leave the office where I was working and play when it was quiet in the afternoon. Other internees would be in their room or at a lecture. I'd finish my work later in the evening. One of the musicians living in the Sefton had noticed I attended Hutchinson camp concerts. He asked me if I would like to play in a concert together with him and his colleagues. I explained I couldn't read music. He came back the next day, with his sheet music and taught me how to read the notes. He gave me homework every night. Eventually I was even good enough to play in a concert once or twice, but then his release came through and that was that."

So whilst his countrymen are sitting in classrooms deciphering English spellings, and losing their German syntax, my Dad is retaining his whilst the tunes in his head turn into notes on a score. He plays duets with his teacher. Brahms, Beethoven, other German composers, flow through his fingertips onto the keys. My father, a Jew, turning memories into music, a language that would keep him connected with his homeland.

2010

The highlight of my Mum's day was when I popped by in the evening, after work. She'd leave a querulous message on my mobile. Bring her a loaf for the freezer; collect a prescription; more tissues; a banana; lemonade, all urgent.

I'd be running through sleet and snow on winter nights to the convenience store or the late night chemist. She'd brew up a bitter black coffee as I swirled into the flat, my cheeks rosy red with cold, snowflakes still glistening on the fur of my Russian trapper hat. Her face would light up when she saw my arms full of shopping, my laptop and a box of continental pastries. We could always enjoy a good *cafe klatch*, a good gossip, over *cafe und kuchen*, coffee and cakes. Now the timing had become erratic, our familiar ritual would sometimes be at supper time, occasionally at midnight, if I stayed over, worried because she wouldn't wake up, even the odd breakfast time instead of a boiled egg, cooked exactly three minutes.

She was impatient for me to sit down and tell stories about work, she'd strain to overcome her deafness and catch my words even though I was shouting at full volume.

I am working with asylum seeker mothers and their babies. My mother peers at the video clips of fresh-faced girls, some of them are still teenagers. Some babies have arrived, the others are still inside.

"What are they talking about?" she asks. She is looking at a picture of the girls laughing together.

"They're talking about names, what they're going to call their children."

My mother's interested. "English names?" she asks.

"Yes, most of them want to give their babies a good English start in life."

The Chinese girl asked us for help choosing because she doesn't speak English yet. Her friend told her about Arthur who was a good neighbour helping everyone on the street. So the baby is now Arthur. The Polish girl couldn't decide if her baby should be Natalya after her mother or Halina after her partner's mother.

"So they call their babies after their mothers and mothers-in-law?"

"Most of them don't have partners. Some babies are a result of rape, some partners were killed and their women have been lucky to escape."

She's silent. She points to a picture of Hilary from Sierra Leone, with her tiny bundle of scarlet and orange cotton tied to her back. "Is she singing?"

"She sings to her baby all the time, the baby never cries."

"And the name?"

"Talia, she says it's after an old lady in her village. She was always kind to Hilary, she was a wise woman, so Hilary hopes if she gives her baby the name, she'll grow up kind and wise too."

"The baby will be kind if the mother is kind," comments my mum removing her specs and rubbing her tired eyes.

"Will they be allowed to stay here?"

"They're waiting to hear from the Home Office if they can stay."

"That'll be a slow business." My mother knew about the bureaucracy around Home Office papers.

She moves closer to the computer because she doesn't see very well and smiles at the mothers gazing tenderly at the babies on the screen. She remembers the two of us, my brother and me, when we were babies.

"You cried; your brother didn't." He was always described as a beautiful baby with curly hair and a perfect complexion. The night he was born they had snuggled together, just the two of them, a coal fire burning at the far end of the long cold room. The sinister drone of the warning sirens sounded as she lay wondering if bombs were going to fall, if they were both going to survive the night.

1976

I receive a parcel from my father. He has made me a present, a cassette in the style of Desert Island Discs, him narrating interspersed with pieces of music. In the narrative interludes he introduces the music, talking about the artists and composers:

Record 1: Artur Rubinstein's performance of Chopin's Larghetto concerto No2 in F Minor, Opus 2L
  "*Rubinstein studied in Berlin; in 1914 he objected to the treatment of the Poles by the German Kaiser's army in the First World War so he left Germany, never to return. He played in Belgian and French border towns where German audiences flocked to hear him. He chose to be an exile.*"

Record 2: Brahms' Hungarian Dances
  "*Many composers are writing music about a particular country, exploring its folk music; but they personally have no relationship with that country at all. Brahms discovered the beauty in Hungarian gypsy music when he moved to Vienna. You see, you can love a ...a new country.*"

Record 3: Bronislav Huberman playing the Brahms violin concerto, which made him famous at the age of 12.
  "*Huberman was a Polish Jew; a prodigy. You know one of his recordings: variations on a nursery song, Op25 by Dohnanyi;* (he sings 'twinkle, twinkle little star' to remind me). *He cancelled all his concert engagements in Germany when Hitler came to power in 1933. He never returned but tirelessly worked to obtain exit visas for Jewish musicians, forming an orchestra of exiles in the desert which was to become Tel-Aviv.*"
  Now, he's playing the rondo from Symphonie Espagnole by Lalo, a Frenchman fascinated by Spanish music.
  Now it's Fritz Kreisler, *who set up soup kitchens for starving Berliners after the First World War.*
  "*I remember him in Berlin, a magnetic figure, who saved Dvorak from poverty by playing his music and giving him the royalties.*"

I listen to Dvorak's Humoresque

"Tauber had to emigrate like so many of us because he had a Jewish father - so he settled here, Europe's loss, England's gain. He was interned too; I went to hear him sing there.

Two years after the war ended, the Vienna Stadts Opera was invited to perform at the Royal Opera House. They invited Tauber as an honorary member to appear in his favourite role, Don Ottario from Don Giovanni, wearing one of the costumes he had carried out of Germany."

2010

My Mum was hardly eating any more. She couldn't be bothered to hold the knife and fork. I was shocked one day as I came through the door to find her holding a plate with one hand and licking it clean, like a dog. Even a spoon was too much effort. I gasped. Was this the person who had taught me how to hold a knife and fork, was this the same person who made us our favourite pudding on our birthday, who allowed us to eat potato pancakes with apple sauce on our knees in front of the fire?

I wiped her blouse clean. I peeled an orange and placed neat little segments on a plate for her. Our roles had been reversed, I had become mother to my mother, I felt desolate.

1976

My father's stories were like music. Singing voices soared above our heads; violin cadenzas carried us on gossamer wings, pianos tinkled like a hundred bells; the notes of a Spanish tango, written by a Frenchman; wild haunting Hungarian gypsy music written by a German. As I listened to the music and the stories that accompanied them my own soul returned to Mittel Europa. The recurring theme of these tales was about exiles for whom England would become home. This procession of musicians walking across our landscape held the beat of Manfred's heart, the rhythm of his life, a language beyond words. Music had been the only constant in the chaos of his changing world.

Written on his cassettes to me were the words:
> *Dein ist mein ganzes Herz! Wo du nicht bist, kann ich nicht sein.'*
>
> *You are my heart's delight; only when you're there, do I exist.*

The Land of Smiles Franz Lehar

2010

I had placed the huge red amaryllis at the foot of her bed. The long green stem was topped by twin orange-red trumpet flower heads with scalloped petals. They looked as if they had been dipped in thick cream. The weight of these large, flamboyant heads was too much for the stem, especially as there was another bulge half way down, the promise of more blooms bursting into life. It was supported with a bamboo cane, all held together with frayed twine.

She said, "Draw it." Together we traced the outline with our fingers in the air, imprinting the trumpet flower shape on our minds, like we did when I was small.

"What will you do for a background?" she asked.

I pulled the aqua curtain across the window. We both agreed the blousy red blooms emerged triumphant against the turquoise.

"I'll paint it tomorrow," I thought. "She can watch me." I pulled away, back into my own life and when I was ready to paint she had turned to stardust.

1976

Manfred was healing himself; his story of exile and humiliation was transformed through the dignity and courage of the procession of musicians. Through the telling of his story he became one of them and I was his witness.

I, a girl of the seventies in the floating skirt, was to be the heir to his memory. He was asking me to inherit his way of describing his identity by performing it through music; otherwise he feared it would be lost forever. He had lost his homeland, the friends of his youth, his future as a German. I was his last chance to remain visible.

He had forced me to step away from my own life and listen through his music. He entrusted me to carry a body of tradition, to the next generation. The cassette in my hands was the mirror on his inner life, and the price he paid for survival.

When he was staying with me he accompanied himself on the piano singing pre-war German pop-songs:

> *Das kommt nur einmal,*
> *das kommt nicht wieder,*
> *das war zu schön*
> *um wahr zu sein*
> *It only happens once*
> *It never comes again*
> *It was too lovely to be true*

2010

She is turned on the bed. She senses me at the door and turns towards me.

"This is difficult," she whispers, "dying is difficult."

"I can see," I reply. "I'm sorry I can't help."

"I could do with my mum to help me," she answers before closing her eyes again and succumbing to what seems like her insides just coming away, both of us had felt we were drowning over the last few weeks, awash with bodily fluid.

"This is how I go out," her last words to me. "You give me nappies now, just as I gave them to you when you came in."

I stand at the threshold watching, she is red raw. I am still tortured by the shame of my ignorance. Urine is acid, it can make you sore. I should have known. I should have been able to help.

Two compassionate black nurses, tending to her gracefully: a dance of the sheets, spreading and folding, turning, wiping and cleaning her so gently. They talk to her; they calm me in soothing low voices,

These women were a gift to my Mum by the state. Thea had feared the state's interference, she feared foreigners in her home and yet we had always been a family of foreigners. At the end she pulled her hand away from mine, unforgiving because I had allowed strangers into her flat.

The night she died I went to collect the amaryllis, switched on her reading lamp, lay on her sofa, and picked up her knitting.

The time had come to become a mother to myself.

Manfred - 1951

Thea - 2010

Chapter 2

If you talk to a man in a language he understands,
that goes to his head. If you talk to him in his own
language, that goes to his heart.
Nelson Mandela

Although my father eventually spoke fluent English, he never lost his Berlin accent. His speech was peppered with Yorkshire expressions and his verbs invariably landed at the end of his sentences. Inside our home he lapsed into German, also Yiddish words were embedded in his stories, connecting him with his grandparents' lives. He immediately became more vivid, more humorous, more himself.

We were raised between two languages. We accessed two cultures. Our parents inhabited an in-between world, tales and troubles, joy and sorrow in both languages. We heard our parents moving from a phrase in one language to a sentence in another. As a child I never knew which language was which. My syntax still betrays my German background. We slipped from one language to the other effortlessly, it didn't matter if it came out wrong. Our endeavour was encouraged and applauded. Mistakes were overlooked in the tacit understanding that we would eventually absorb a correct way. We heard it around us and understood. Eventually we spoke.

There was no careful puzzling over verb declension or learning lists of vocabulary. My brother and I picked out words and strung them together, sometimes we picked out words that sounded funny, made us laugh and turned them into nonsense language, a code between the two of us.

German is the language of my nursery rhymes; it has seeped through my skin. I speak with an English accent. I soften the harsh guttural sounds, I lose the diminutives. I keep the cadences, I keep the phrases. The second language made me more attentive to my first. I search for words with different nuances. I notice the space between words. It's a different quality of listening.

We had often been amazed when one word could mean two entirely different things. Zug means train, but it also means draught.

"I'm sitting in the train," my father would remark if he wanted me to close the door.

I discovered that we could be having a conversation entirely meaning the opposite to each other; we could both be right and be making a mistake at the same time. There's no clear right or wrong way, I learned as a little girl, turn the kaleidoscope and there are infinite ways of looking at the world.

We were driven through Europe, where we realised there were other languages, not just English, German and Hebrew in prayer books. French, Italian, Spanish…where should we start?

My dad kept saying, "You must have at least one more language."

"Why?"

"You never know when you might need it. You don't know when you might have to go, to settle somewhere else, you need to earn your living wherever you are."

So we learned French in school, properly structured, reciting prepositions and negatives, but we never spoke it the same, it came from our head, neatly packaged and ordered somewhere inside our brains, German rested in our hearts, absorbed through our pores, through cuddles and smiles, through shouting, through sorrow and happiness.

I had another language to play with as a child, wrapped around me like a blanket, the language of favourite stories, the language used to lift me up to hug and kiss me, the diminutive reminding me I was the littlest, the sweetest and the hope of the next generation. I still carry that language inside me, a jewel that suddenly sparkles as words and phrases learnt long ago jump into the light, illuminating my way through Europe.

They patiently explained the meaning of words, phrases, puns. Johnny and I were weaving their stories of a German life together with our own English stories. The continental characters of our childhood used language theatrically and we turned them into cartoon characters. We mimicked their exaggerated expressions:

"entsückend"   (enchanting)   *"grossartig"*
(Brilliant). *"grausam"* (Grotesque)

They often implored and exclaimed to God. *"Ach du lieber Gott","Gott in Himmel", "mein Gott"*, echoing a more fervent religious past when blessings of gratitude were constantly being uttered. Then they had been part of a community, their individual dreams and desires subsumed in the rules and rituals of orthodox Jewish life. They had escaped Nazi Germany. Each individual had a separate story of survival. Here they found themselves without their old ties and community, a random collection of lost souls from somewhere east of Calais, in the direction of Mittel Europa.

Johnny and I copied these exclamations in loud theatrical voices in our shared conversations. We were the threads that tied them all together, our existence gave them a future. We teased them whilst they struggled with the idiosyncrasies of English and the impossibility of pronouncing words correctly. Aunty Frieda talked of "pluffing a field", bemused at our hysterical laughter. My father talked of finding a "sheep pension."

From the back of the car one of our voices would call out:
"Daddy, will there be sheep staying at the pension"
The other voice:
"Do EWE know when we'll get there?"
We'd snort and chuckle at German signs:
Ausfahrt, Einfahrt, Überfahrt , Unterfahrt and above all *Himmelfahrt,* farting all the way up to heaven .

We lived in no-man's land, England outside and somewhere else inside, partly Germany partly an idiosyncratic émigré country invented in our own heads through listening to our parents' descriptions of life before. I projected myself into their European world through the images and anecdotes they gave me, through the furniture they brought with them, the music they danced to, the 1930s paste jewellery they pinned to their clothes. Everything from the thirties became exotic and unattainable to me; it became the focus of my aspiration

Chapter 3

Background

A dash of the Rhine and the Oder found its way into
our grim runnel - "t'mucky beck."
J.B. Priestly - An English Journey

Thea was and wasn't English. Her father, Eugene, had been a successful mill owner in South Yorkshire. He was born in Bad Homburg, the second son of a large family. His widowed mother managed two hotels, earning enough to support her eldest son while he studied medicine. The younger children started work at fourteen. Eugene had been apprenticed in a factory where his workmates had pinned him down, forcing him to eat pork sausage, calling him dirty Jew. She bought him a one-way ticket to New York.

In 1880, aged16, he set sail alone for a new world. He worked in a chocolate factory, at first eating as many as he could, but after a few weeks he was nauseated by the heavy sweet smell and worked instead as a window dresser in Macy's department store. He enjoyed draping and pinning the woven fabrics and found many were made in the north of England. He was homesick for Europe and returned after a year. As he could speak English he travelled to Yorkshire and found work in a shoddy mill.

Shoddy was poor quality wool, made by recycling rags, shredding them into fibres and mixing them with bits of new wool. Small groups of pioneering Germans, including Ashkenazi Jews, were establishing themselves in Lancashire and Yorkshire, at the heart of the wool and cotton industries. Some traded with America, but Eugene Weiss concentrated on business with Europe. He travelled there regularly, collecting woollen rags, and was able to communicate with his clients in several languages.

During the First World War his business flourished, providing wool for blankets and uniforms, later he sold raw woollen material in central Europe. The English textile business declined in the 1960s with the arrival of synthetic fibres from the Far East.

Eugene became a Yorkshire man with an accent from the Rhine, the wide river where ships travelled up and down carrying their cargo through Europe. He married my grandmother, Margareta, on New Year's Eve 1900. I still have the gold and black cross-stitched tablecloth from her trousseau, sewn by her sisters.

My grandmother came from a family of six children. Her father was a scrap metal merchant. The three daughters sat at home knitting and stitching, singing Schubert lieder and waiting for husbands. In my box of treasures I have their photograph; all, pinned-up hair and starched collars, standing around their severe-looking mother, holding a walking stick to steady her hand shaking with Parkinson's disease. Lucy, the eldest, has a shiny, scrubbed little face with a cloud of frizzy hair. Frieda, the youngest, a spinster destined to be her mother's carer, faces inward, looking towards her mother's trembling hand. Margareta glares at the camera. She was always bored, she told me, desperate to get out of the house, to do something, not just wait for a husband.

"You're so lucky. You can have the same education as a boy and do anything you want." She was old when she said this, her hands, covered with liver spots, always busy with embroidery or knitting. Her eldest brother Richard had been to university, to become a doctor. She wanted to study too.

"No," said her father. "Who's heard of a female doctor? Educated girls don't find husbands easily, and men don't want clever women. You stay at home with your sisters."

1900

My grandmother was 23 when Eugene proposed. Thrilled, she packed her trunks and set sail for England with hardly a backward glance. They were the early pioneers in our family, secular Jews, the first to become English. It was fourteen years before the First World War and they could choose their new country and nationality.

Margarete, always known as Gretchen, remained loyal to her German roots as well as grafting on Englishness with a Sunday roast, cold meat on Monday, minced meat rissoles on Tuesday and Shepherd's Pie on Wednesday.

When I was young I was perched on the edge of her worktop and helped her stuff chunks of meat into the top of her old, steel mincer, slowly turning the handle until red worms wriggled through the mesh and plopped on to the plate underneath. They were moulded into rissoles with wet hands, dipped into egg and flour and arranged on a wooden board, ready to be browned in the sizzling frying pan.

She taught me how to make her English puddings - treacle pudding swimming in extra golden syrup. She made baked apples, stuffed with dried fruit and honey, rice pudding with jam, semolina flavoured with grated orange. They would cook in a blue-edged enamel bowl carefully lowered into a large saucepan of bubbling water. She showed me how to separate eggs, tipping the sunshine yolk from one half shell into the other, allowing the white stream, reminiscent of snot and spit, fall into the bowl. We competed to see who could beat sauces and custards with the balloon whisk, faster and faster so that the eggs wouldn't curdle whilst inhaling the aroma of warm milk, citrus zest and vanilla.

Her German-ness emerged with the goose at Christmas, accompanied with red cabbage, sweet and sour with vinegar and brown sugar, sautéed with raisins and apples, all to be eaten on Christmas Eve.

My Gran and I also baked together. We made meringues like exploding white peonies. I sandwiched a blob of whipped cream between two shells. The first bite would leave a cream moustache on the upper lip. She taught me to make biscuits, inventing different flavours. We sliced slivers of orange peel and crystallised ginger, adding a little syrup here, a sprinkle of cinnamon there, the smell of ground cloves, the crunch of chopped hazelnuts. We made dough with swirls of chocolate and vanilla, and shaped marbled little cookie balls with a suggestion of icing. We cut hearts, stars and scalloped circles out of dough, painted them with egg yolk to make them shiny. These trays of tiny biscuits were whipped in and out of the oven as I became a German baker.

She crocheted lace curtains to hang in the windows instead of nets. She read English newspapers, English novels from Daphne du Maurier's Rebecca to Emily Bronte's Wuthering Heights. But her poetry was German. In the afternoons when we both lay on opposite ends of the sofa resting and reading, she'd pick up her volume of Heine or Schiller. I'd close my eyes, and half dozing would listen to the words floating above my head, whilst sucking her aniseed balls or chewing a Pontefract cake.

1914

> *They do not want to pass for Jews, although every*
> *child in Bradford knows them to be Jews."*
> Jewish Chronicle (11 August1865)

Eugene and Gretchen lived through the First World War in Dewsbury. They were isolated from their families in Germany and were mistrusted in Dewsbury for their nationality and German accents, although they were no longer German, having been naturalised. Eugene bought encyclopaedias and classical German literature to read when he retired but died before he had the chance. He kept tadpoles in the bath, rats in a cage and even a squirrel. He sat on the wall of his house, swinging his short legs puffing at his pipe and chatting to children on the street. He described himself as an Englishman but he never met his English grandchildren. I believe he was a European.

Their son attended an English boarding school to eliminate traces of German-ness and Jewishness. Gretchen suffered two miscarriages and a third baby, Norman, was stillborn. He rests in an unmarked part of the orthodox Jewish cemetery in Gildersome, West Yorkshire. Jewish law forbade headstones for babies and there was no mourning period. She wasn't allowed to take flowers to the grave but she smuggled them in surreptitiously, forget-me-nots wrapped in her coat, even when she was old and I accompanied her, picking up pebbles to put on my grandfather's grave.

In 1916 my mother was born at home with a shock of red hair. Her father was excited when he registered her birth. He gave her a boy's name by mistake; Theo, should have been Thea. It was an easy birth, at midday, when the winter sun makes the icicles sparkle on the windowsill, turning them into multi-coloured prisms.

1919

The three-year-old is playing in the garden. She has a mass of tumbling auburn curls tied back from her face with an enormous pink ribbon. She's only been playing out for five minutes and her white dress is already grubby. She has long black socks and brown ankle boots fastened with tiny buttons. The doll's table she drags into the middle of the lawn is almost as big as she is. She carefully places the tiny teacups and then runs round the table a few times, chased by her small fox terrier. They sit down on the step together and she tells him, "Scamp, you have to sit nicely at the tea table". He gives her hot little face a lick and runs off into the bushes.

"Never mind, I'll invite my friends for tea instead. Nitchymitch, Nitchymitch." She runs off, brings back a large cushion and places it near the table. "One sugar or two?" she says to the cushion. "Two. Have you seen Sand on his way up? Dear me he's always late." She runs off and brings another cushion. "There you are Sand, have you been a good boy? Have you seen Scamp? He's been very naughty as usual."

She pours pretend tea out of her miniature teapot. She looks in the rhododendron bushes for the little dog who has run panting in the heat to the house, hoping for a scratch behind the ears, a bowl of water and a quiet snooze.

Thea listens, she hears her mother talking to the little dog, the sounds are coming from the next door garden, she can hear her Aunty Mela serving proper tea, the clink of the cups, the two women are chatting and laughing, the German words float through the garden. The little girl sits on the ground listening. "Nitchmitch, nitchy mish, mitchy nish," she whispers into the cushion mimicking the German sounds. She was always playing alone and she remembered watching the children with funny shaped legs with rickets, she said. She longed to join in their games when she went to the shop with her mum to buy milk.

Gretchen spent a lot of time alone with my mum. It was difficult to make friends because she was German. She sewed clothes, she knitted, she dressed my mum up and took photographs printing them in the little pantry off her kitchen. She touched up the photographs by hand in coloured inks, My mum stood alone, holding her toy rabbit, dressed in a teddy bear fur coat with a muff (which I wore many years later in Leeds snow).

Her mother was in the pantry she had turned into a dark room, totally absorbed by the magic of images slowly appearing in the tray of solution, tweezers in hand ready to hang the print on the line to dry.

Thea was two when World War One ended. In 1920 Uncle Richard arrived to visit. He hugged his little niece, removed his Homburg hat and sat down for a tea party with her imaginary friends. He felt nervous in Dewsbury, conspicuous in his patterned Berlin suit, lilac shirt and stiff cravat, with his monocle and silver-topped cane amongst the Yorkshire men with their flat caps and incomprehensible accents. Most of his time in England was spent reading Struwelpeter, in German, to Thea until she didn't know whether to squeal in delight or fear.

He told stories of his work as a doctor in the German army, working in a field hospital where operations were performed without anaesthetic. More German Jews fought in World War I than any other ethnic, religious or political group in Germany. Twelve thousand died for their country. His stories were in vivid contrast to his current life in Berlin in the heady days of the Weimar republic, jazz music floating out of bars, sexual experimentation and a whiff of cocaine.

Eugene and Margarete Weiss

1922

Thea's new project was knitting an entire wardrobe for Nellie, her porcelain doll. She used the strands of wool her mother and aunt gave her from their own knitting projects. A loud bell made her jump. She climbed on a footstool and stood on tiptoe to reach the large wind-up telephone attached to the wall.

"Heckmondwike 2-1," she lisped, clutching the large receiver in her hands. It was her father from his office at the shoddy mill in Heckmondwike.

"Tell Mummy to start packing, we're off tomorrow," he said in English.   Gretchen called from the kitchen in German, "Tell him not to be late, his dinner's in the oven." They were the only family in Dewsbury to have a telephone.

Several times a year Eugene set off by car to buy rags, crossing the North Sea at Harwich and driving from the Hook of Holland to Berlin, continuing to Munich, Vienna, Prague and Budapest. Gretchen and Thea stood on the harbour edge watching their car being winched through the air on to the boat. In Berlin he rented a different flat for each visit. After the First World War they lived mainly in Berlin, seven year old Thea started school there. She grew up speaking two languages, the child of immigrant parents in England, a child with a German peer group in Berlin. She had always spoken German within the family and as an adult couldn't remember which language came first.

She had visited her grandparents, now retired in Berlin. She was allowed to skip down the long gloomy corridors with their faint odour of camphor. She was always hushed, everyone whispering not to disturb her sick uncle resting behind large, etched glass double-doors.

They kept her china doll, Nellie, in tissue paper and she was allowed to play quietly in front of the old tiled stove for two hours every afternoon as sunlight faded through the large windows until she could hardly distinguish her grandparent's faces fondly watching her with beloved Nellie on the rug. The curtains would eventually be drawn to enfold her in darkness.

Large oil paintings of her grandparents hung on either side of the fireplace in my grandmother's house. My great-grandfather, Philip Calman, looked kindly and whiskered. He lived in Stettin, once Poland, later to become Germany. Hitler took respite here after the First World War. It was where he decided to hate the Jews. I used to wonder if it was all my family's fault. Maybe Philip Calman, walking down the Street one spring day, unwittingly curdled the mind and spirit of Adolf Hitler.

Anna Calman, my great grandmother looked forbidding, encased in her gilt frame. She fixed me with a stern gaze. Her face was framed with neat rolls and high lace collar, her lips mean and hardly present. I often stood in front of the fire gazing at their portraits, as I warmed the back of my legs. I stuck my tongue out at her, occasionally, testing whether I would be struck down by a bolt of lightning.

Berlin

Thea's parents rented a fourth floor flat in the centre of Berlin. She ran up the steps and inspected the generous rooms. She was delighted when Gretchen flung open the tall French windows and revealed a wide balcony overlooking the busy street. Her father burst through the door carrying a tortoise that they both fussed over, building its home in a packing case lined with shredded newspaper.

Her parents enrolled her in the Lesslerschule at Roseneck. This was in leafy Grunewald, a predominantly Jewish area. Toni Lessler, the head teacher, had developed educational programmes for delicate children and later, for overseas pupils. She registered her school with English exam boards ensuring that her pupils would reach a level of English to enable them to study abroad. After Hitler became chancellor in 1933, she enrolled mainly Jewish girls and encouraged her pupils to become proficient at English in case they needed to emigrate. Now there must be few Jews left in Grunewald, just a few street names as a reminder.

Thea's first day at school was her seventh birthday. Gretchen accompanied her by tram through the snow to the converted mansion, set back from the road with a wide sweeping lawn. She was clutching the traditional giant cone of sweets to celebrate the rite of passage.

This was the year of German hyper-inflation. At the beginning of term Gretchen pulled down the brown leather suitcase they used to carry their belongings between Dewsbury and Berlin. She went to the bank and withdrew armfuls of paper notes, that term's school fees, which she stuffed into the suitcase. She accompanied Thea on the bus to school and handed over the suitcase. Frau Lessler quickly carried the suitcase straight to the bank before the money inflated again.

Thea Weiss (White) sat next to Edzia Schwartz (Black). The two little girls, one with bright auburn curls, the other with jet black plaits, eyed each other with suspicion for a couple of days before becoming best friends. Thea struggled to speak correct German so that her class mates wouldn't laugh at her. Edzia helped her practice her German pronunciation, verb endings and spellings. They had been born in the First World War and were to lose each other in the next war. Thea with her baby surrounded by a loving family in Leeds, Edzia with her baby watching Tel-Aviv grow out of the desert in Israel, trying to understand why her family had disappeared. They were reunited by the Red Cross in 1948; each had been searching for the other. They were still corresponding when they were old women, spidery German handwriting, dog-eared photographs of smiling grandchildren and descriptions of the book they were currently reading, but not a word about the past.

Thea was soon old enough to take the tram unaccompanied and stay with her severe grandmother and Aunty Frieda when her parents went back to England.

A podgy teenager, unkempt red hair freckles and a disarming grin, she loved school and worked hard, After Edzia transferred to the academic Gymnasium to prepare for exams, Thea's new friend was Ruth, artistic and a year older. After school they went to Thea's, sitting on the balcony, painting and drawing. They drank milk and ate large slabs of chocolate cake baked by my grandmother, sunshine lit up the pink geraniums in the window boxes, high above the street.

She had become a German teenager, the first to dive into the chilly Wannsee when the spring arrived. She splashed and swam in the lake every day after school, across the water from the house where meetings to decide the final solution were held.

1934 The rise of Hitler

Thea had tea at her Uncle Richard's spacious flat, near Bayerischeplatz, with its high ceilings, etched glass double doors leading from one room to the next. She was feeding crumbs of cake from her china plate to little Max, Richard's Dachshund, sitting on his hind legs waiting hopefully for scraps. They were chatting:

"Thea you must continue your studies, you could do many things with your life."

"What?" she said, "What could I do?"

"Well, you're fluent in two languages, you could be an interpreter."

She bent down to cuddle Max now snoozing at her feet.

"Maybe you could write in English papers some of the things happening to us here in Germany."

"Sounds boring," she mutters, folding Max's silky ear round her finger.

"Let's go for a walk," said Richard, putting on his hat and carefully buttoning up his overcoat.

They walked through the surrounding streets, passing the Muchenerstrasse synagogue. There was shouting and scuffles outside the Jewish shops as Brownshirts stood outside to prevent Germans from entering. Thea took her uncle's arm, she could barely grasp what was happening. They watched as one of the soldiers who'd been hurling abuse at the shop owner; daubed a star on the window in yellow paint.

"Why are they doing that?" she asked. "They'll go to prison for attacking those shops won't they?"

Richard realised his English niece had not understood the Nuremburg laws which had already banned Jews from working in the public sector, part of a plan to make the Jews "Untermenschen", sub-humans. Richard had not yet told his family that he was no longer allowed to treat German citizens in his clinic, only Jews.

By now, many believed Hitler's accusations that the 1923 hyperinflation had been caused by an international Jewish attempt to destroy Germany. These violent attacks were condoned and encouraged by the state. They passed another shop. This time a soldier was writing Jude (Jew) on the window in big letters, the owner was standing watching in his shirtsleeves.

Max chose this moment to roll on his back, rocking from side-to-side, asking for a tummy tickle. Thea bent down to oblige. Richard watched his niece and his little sausage dog ecstatically waving all his paws in the air. How could he tell her that he had decided to send his dog away; the Nazi party had passed a law forbidding Jews to own pets.

She felt his hand on her shoulder.

"You won't be allowed to attend a university or gymnasium here, Thea. You have a British passport, get out now, quickly, and build a new life for yourself in England, you're young, all this will get worse, and who knows where it will end up."

Eugene Weiss was watching too, his experiences all those years before, as an apprentice had come back to haunt him, only much worse. The Nuremberg Laws now decreed that Jews lost their right to be German citizens, marriage between Jews and non-Jews was forbidden. It was after this law that the violence against the Jews openly started. Those that could

49

pay fines for racially induced fabricated crimes were allowed to leave the country. Many could not and many shops refused to sell food to those who remained.

When Thea was sixteen Frau Lessler suggested that she sat the German state exam that would allow her university entrance; she gave her extra coaching.

"Thea, you should study, I'm sure you'll pass easily," she said. "The exams are taking place in a school near Uhlandstrasse. I want you to go and although I would like to come I don't think it's helpful if I accompany you. If we emphasise that you're English, with luck the authorities won't notice you're Jewish. If I come with you, it's the only thing they'll think about."

Thea crossed Berlin alone on exam day, satchel nonchalantly balanced on her hip, squinting in the sunlight because her auburn curls kept falling into her eyes. She lit a cigarette as she crossed the road against the lights, and was promptly stopped by a German soldier. "Oops, sorry," she said, with a grin, deeply inhaling a puff of her cigarette, "I'm English you see, I don't understand German." She released the nicotine smoke through her nostrils, blowing it in his face and sauntered off.

Thea believed her Englishness made her invincible. She had a British passport in her pocket and took every opportunity to flaunt her disregard for the rules imposed by the Nazis. When she was stopped for her papers, she just laughed and waved her passport in the air. A month later she received her exam results; she had passed. She excitedly told her parents she would now transfer to a gymnasium like her friends and work for her Abitur ('A' level equivalent). "I could become a lawyer like Edzia," she burbled. "I think I might like to do psychology, there's this man, Freud, in Vienna,, my teachers told me he has all sorts of theories about how our mind works..."

Her father explained that it was impossible for her to transfer to a German gymnasium, they were finished with Germany. She could continue her studies in England.

Thea had always driven back and forth from Dewsbury to Berlin. Now she's German, now she's English. Now she's not allowed to be German, even have a German boyfriend. The

Jewish thing was hardly an issue in her mind. Now she's sixteen. Suddenly her father tells her they're leaving Germany forever.

"I'm German, I belong here, my friends are here."

She had never been to school in England, never had the opportunity to make English friends.

"It's not fair," she said. "You drag me over here to become German, I had to learn a new language …now I'm enjoying myself you're trying to force me to become English again…"

There is a pause whilst Eugene searches for words to explain his own fears without scaring her.

"I hate you, I belong here. Ich bin ein Berliner". The door slams shut, she stays out all night.

A week later they leave for England. Thea is heartbroken.

1937

Thea refused to enrol in an English school, with their stuffy rules and disgusting uniforms with straw hats, braying schoolgirls waving hockey sticks. She found herself trying to understand the administrative systems in the office at Longfield Mills, Eugene's shoddy mill in Heckmondwike. She hated it and was aching for her carefree teenage Berlin life, where everything was exciting. She was 16, like her mother before she felt stifled; she was losing her newly found agency. Her father was forcing her into a life she longed to reject; she blamed him. She didn't understand Hitler was forcing her father to flee from the life she had always taken for granted. Dewsbury was dead, there were no cafes, no U-bahn stations, apparently no boyfriends.

After work she caught the bus into Leeds tottering in her high heels. Leeds is not Berlin, but there are pubs and shops, still no cafes. She hung around Whitelock's bar with her older brother and his friends, supping beer, chain smoking and eventually, staggering home drunk. She stood shivering at the bus stop on Briggate, waiting for the late night bus home to Dewsbury. When she alighted she turned her collar up against the damp Yorkshire night. A policeman watched her swinging her bag as she picked her way over the cobbles towards their big house on Springfield Terrace.

"I'll walk up street with thee - you don't want to be walking there alone this time of night." She scowled at him.

"I'm used to going everywhere alone." He detected a slight accent.

"Not here luv," he answered good-humouredly. "I'm not letting a young girl like you walk alone this time of night."

They walked up the street in silence. She did smile at him at the gate. "Thank you."

He was nice, she thought, kind. She'd never admitted how her stomach had lurched when she'd been approached by one of those brown-shirted policemen in Berlin, so sharp, so unfriendly. She'd never let anyone know she'd been a bit scared.

Chapter 4

Hello, Manfred Gornitzky

1937

Round the corner from KDW, the exclusive department store, a stone's throw from the U-bahn station, Wittenburg Platz, is Gornitzky's shop on Passauerstrasse. It is a June day; Manfred is sitting in the pavement cafe next to his father's shop. He orders another coffee cognac. He sells their home-manufactured soap and shampoo.

He lights a cigarette, sits back, shades his eyes, squinting into the sunlight to see if his girlfriend is coming. He is rolling his sleeves up when she appears, breathless, by his side.

"I'm sorry Manfred, I had an audition, and I think I might have done well." He was hardly listening. Standing up he took her large bag off her shoulder, breathed in her fresh soapy smell and longed to touch the stray auburn curl escaping at the nape of her neck.

"A cafe cognac?" he asked. She nodded and sat down solemnly.

"We must talk."

"We must kiss first," he said, anxious at the earnest expression on her face.

"No Manfred..."

"Look, I've got Hulda's keys." He jangled a bunch of keys in front of her, the keys to his aunt's flat above the shop where

53

he would arrange romantic trysts whilst she was at work. She was processing a deluge of emigration applications.

"Manfred, it's got to stop."

He pretended he hadn't heard, reaching over the table to arrange escaping wisps of hair.

"Manfred."

"Why so sudden?"

"You know why. You've read the latest Nuremberg law. We could be imprisoned for being together."

"How would anyone know?"

"Just look at you, you don't look like a typical Aryan."

He didn't respond, she was right, his crisp black hair and large eyes identified him as a Jew immediately.

"They know my name, the brownshirts, they might recognise my face from the movie, besides you know they make random checks on the street, we're together, they look at our identity passes and..."

"I'll risk it."

"Manfred..."

"I'm not afraid of them."

"You don't get it, do you? They say they're going to make it a capital offence for Jews to contaminate Aryan women; you could be imprisoned, even worse."

Worse was beyond 22-year-old Manfred's imagination. He pointed to his camera on the table.

"I've shot some footage at the opera; I thought you'd like to see."

She didn't answer, took a cigarette out of the leather case, he leaned over to light it. The sun had begun to go down; the café was in the shade, it felt colder.

"You know I don't really care about being Jewish, I just care about being with you."

"Manfred, I do, it's too much, even my parents want us to stop. They think you should go away."

"Away from you?"

"Not just that, away from here; they don't think you're safe."

"What, just because I was beaten up by brownshirts last week? That was my fault?"

"You shouldn't get beaten up because you are filming on the street, it's not right."

"They didn't get the camera anyway, I threw it in the bushes and after they finished with me they'd forgotten." He touched the yellow bruise on his temple.

"I didn't give you the camera to put you in danger."

"You're saying just being with me is putting me in danger?"

"Yes." She was standing now.

"Go away Manfred; go before it's too late."

"Alicia I got tickets for the opera...just you and me..."

She shook her head, she was blurred, and she was gone.

Manfred sat for a long time watching the shadows lengthening on the street. He watched his father close down the blinds of the shop. He drank both cafe cognacs and let himself in to Hulda's flat. He stood at the window overlooking the grassy open space. Two little girls were chasing each other, one with long black pigtails, the other in a pink dress. They sat down on a bench to catch their breath. He saw the girl with pigtails nudge her friend and pointed to a bench along the path. They got up and slowly walked to the new bench, they sat down. It was the yellow bench, with a label on it: Jews only

He kicks the table leg, throws the chair across the room, and wipes away tears with his shirtsleeve. He opens the lid of his aunt's piano, starts playing 1920s love songs, the tango 'Last night you came to me in my dreams'. He progresses to a Brahms lullaby and by the time he has completed a chirpy Chopin waltz, the stone in his chest is dissolving.

What must he do? He can't get a visa; it costs too much. Where would he go? He can only speak German. He watches two brownshirts crossing the park. How can he hate a place and love it at the same time? How would he earn his living? He has no portable skills; he dropped out of school before exams, too boring. What about his parents? Their savings were dwindling rapidly, trade had dropped after the Nazi onslaught on Jewish shops, they couldn't afford tickets to emigrate. He sticks his head out of the window to inhale the smell of Berlin in the summertime. The little girls are still on the yellow bench playing patacake. He slams the window shut. He'll enrol at the ORT tomorrow.

Manfred's mother Edith Gornitzky, Mama, had been raised in Gustrau, one of six children. All the sisters worked and her brother had become a respected lawyer. Edith was the eldest, maybe closest to her father and, as a result, felt responsible for continuing a traditional religious lifestyle. She kept Kosher and lived within an orthodox framework.

Manfred's beloved grandfather was Rabbi Bucki.

In a small town like Gustrow this meant he not only acted as the local rabbi but performed all the roles necessary for the Jewish population to lead an observant life. He was trained to slaughter animals in the kosher manner. He was also the Hazan (cantor) leading both the melodies and providing the spiritual strength of the services in the synagogue.

On Shabbos evening there was always an extra place set at the table, to welcome a stranger. Friday nights (Shabbos) in Leeds, in the 1950s, my mother lit the candles and set the empty place, my father always said:

"We must have extra food ready, in case. I was a stranger once, there will always be someone seeking asylum who needs feeding."

Israeli students at Leeds University came and, after the Hungarian Uprising of 1956, a number of Hungarian refugees arrived to eat the Shabbos meal with us.

The parents of our grandfather, Herman Gorniztky, Papa, came from Grodno, Lithuania. Since the eighteenth century, these Jews had been allowed freedom to move from town to town in order to trade, but not allowed to settle in one place. There had been a strong Zionist presence in Grodno as well as Jewish labour movements, the 'Bund'. They organized Jewish self-defence in 1903 and 1907, avenging the bloodshed that resulted from the pogroms at Bialystok. My great-grandparents Gornitzky left Lithuania between 1872 and 1892 to avoid conscription into the Russian army. Pushing their belongings in a cart, they walked to Nancy in Eastern France. Eventually they moved to north Germany, first to Hamburg and later to Gustrow. Papa was the only member of the family who chose to take German nationality. As a result, he alone was conscripted into the German army and served as a medical orderly in World War One.

The Gorniztky/Bucki family had worked in religious professions or as traders, moving from town to town as generations of Ashkenazi Jews before them. They always lived hand to mouth, buying and selling. Jews were denied access to the professions until the 1900s in Germany and even then were not allowed to enter the civil service. My family repeated this pattern after they escaped Nazi persecution and landed in Salford 1938.

The ORT was an international Jewish training movement, originally Russian. They were now providing professional and vocational training for adults to equip them with practical skills as they prepared for immigration. Manfred decided to study chemistry. He'd learn how to make kosher shampoo and household cleaning material. After all there were Jewish people everywhere in the world; he could find somewhere else to belong. He ran down the stairs, he'll talk to his little brother, Kurt, currently working in their father's factory learning to make soap. They could work this out; they could start somewhere new together. It would be an adventure. We'll go to the sun, he thought.

He ran past the café, blocking out the memory of his meeting with Alicia. To keep himself calm he re-ran the Chopin waltz in his head. No crying, be tough, action!

His Dad will have counted the takings by now; they'll walk home together, just in time before Shabbos comes in. He'll wait till the candles are lit and the blessings said. He'll talk to his parents over the meal, stress the urgency, and see if they will consider emigration. How would they learn a new language he pondered? To him they both seemed inseparable from the first floor flat on the Kantstrasse. Home was this Jewish neighbourhood of Berlin, the flat, his Mum in the kitchen and Sabbath coming in. He couldn't visualise how else life could be.

The net closes in

Eugene knew there would be a war. He decided to make a last trip to Europe and retrieve as many assets as possible. Gretchen was worrying about her ageing mother. So they all returned to Berlin. Thea stayed with her grandmother and Frieda. She slept on a camp bed in Frieda's room. She was supposed to be tucked up in bed at ten pm. This was worse than Dewsbury. She waited until Frieda was snoring and carefully climbed out of the window, holding the straps of her high heels between her teeth, the flared skirt of her dress tucked into her knickers. A dog barked as she landed on the gravel pathway. Frieda woke, and called through the window. Thea ignored her and ran off down the street.

She's thrilled to be back, sitting in a Berlin cafe, with a crowd of her friends, Jewish young people, sharing cafe-cognac and discussing how they would get out of Germany. They were making plans, learning different languages, young people excited by the prospect of change and adventure. My mother always described those conversations without any sense of impending danger, the confidence of youth and ignorance.

"Did you mix with Christians too?" I used to ask naively. She never said "We weren't allowed." She never mentioned the Nuremberg laws, she also never mentioned that she wouldn't dare date a boy who wasn't Jewish, that it was against the law, soon to become a capital offence, 'intent to taint Aryan blood'.

She enrolled at the ORT school where Manfred was studying chemistry, writing formulae down in a little black book. Thea was studying beauty therapy and massage and enrolled in a chemistry class to analyse the ingredients in Grace Beauty products that she hoped to sell in the future.

He noticed her, another ginger, and invited her out for a coffee. A few days later like many other Berliner teenagers she took the metro to the Bahnhof am Zoo and stood under the big clock waiting for her date. My father sauntered up to her in his dark coat and Fedora. He brought his precious cine camera and she blew cigarette smoke into the lens as he filmed her in the Cafe Unter den Linden. She told him about her mother's photos and how she had converted the pantry into a dark room in the Dewsbury house.

"Dewsbury, where's that?" he asked.

"Oh, just a little place, where I used to live, in England." She was English, he realised, she already had her papers, she was free to leave.

Thea was reluctant to recognise that the third Reich was gaining momentum. Eugene saw that life for the Jews was intolerable and so he was finally closing his business contacts in Europe.

Manfred bought tickets for the Berlin State opera. The Nazi laws were emphatic about Jews neither attending nor participating in artistic or cultural events. They went, but felt uncomfortable. In better times he had been an extra. They would post the name of the next production and he would queue all night at the stage door. They would pick the first, 20, 40 100 young people to participate in the Opera. My father knew many arias in German and some in Italian. He would sing them in the bath, whilst shaving, when he was driving us through Europe and occasionally to lull us to sleep. He was surprised he wasn't easily understood in Italy. He would gesticulate and come out with random snatches of Italian verse from the Opera and expect them to understand his wish to buy an ice cream.

He bought tickets for the Berlin Olympics. The opening ceremony was a spectacular display of Nazi pageantry. There was a never-ending procession of Brown shirts, SS men and Hitler Youth all carrying long red swastika banners and torches. When the then chancellor, Adolf Hitler, entered the specially built stadium an orchestra played the Nazi anthem and all 110,000 spectators rose to their feet giving him the Nazi salute. My mum and dad held hands and crept away quietly. The anti-Semitic posters such as "Jews not welcome here," that had littered Germany before the games, were carefully concealed. Newspapers inciting hatred against the Jews were no longer on sale – the Nazis did everything to camouflage their attacks on the Jews. Jesse Owens, an African-American, described by the Nazis as racially inferior, won four gold medals in the 100m, 200m, long jump and 4 x 100m relay. Hitler refused to place the gold medal around Owens's neck.

Thea wandered through the streets of Berlin alone on Yom Kippur (Day of Atonement). She went to the Friedenstempel (peace synagogue) to listen to sermons by Rabbi Joachim Prinz which addressed young people on contemporary issues. Prinz later emigrated to the US and continued to preach against racism in the US. He marched with Martin Luther King in 1963 and spoke these words prior to the famous I have a dream speech:

> *A great people (in Germany) which had created a great civilization had become a nation of silent onlookers. They remained silent in the face of hate, in the face of brutality and in the face of mass murder. America must not become a nation of onlookers. America must not remain silent.*

Thea bumped into Manfred, who secretly, not to offend his parents, had previously attended the Fasanenstrasse synagogue, also a liberal congregation, under Rabbi Leo Beck. They both were drawn to Prinz's sermons urging his young followers to leave Germany. Thea watched as the Torah was carried around the synagogue; she watched the children carefully undress the scrolls. The music echoed the laments of the ghettos, written within Jewish communities over a hundred years ago. She watched Manfred lower his head and touch the scroll with the fringes of his tallit. As he kissed the fringe he turned his head, their eyes met,

"Stay with me," he whispered. She assumed this was a marriage proposal.

1937

Farewell Germany

My mother described her Berlin courting days and visiting her future mother-in-law, Mama, every Friday. They went shopping for the Shabbos meal. The chicken was complete with feathers. It had to be a mature hen with un-laid eggs that would be added to the soup, just before serving. Thea watched Mama pluck the chicken, deftly pulling all the feathers out, then holding the naked carcass over the gas flame to scorch the pinfeathers left behind. It gave off an acrid smell. Soup-greens and a beef bone strengthened the flavour. The chicken was cut into pieces using poultry shears and lowered into the simmering broth. My mother was never sure which cloth to use to dry the dishes. She was not used to the rules of Kashrut in the kitchen. Mama also baked the challah, mixing the dough and covering it with a large cloth so it could rise. Later she would punch it down, roll it out and plait it. She brushed the loaf with egg yolk using a large feather from the plucked chicken. Finally she sprinkled it with poppy seeds and put it in the oven.

Thea set the table whilst the aroma of yeasty baking bread filled the kitchen. She watched Mama, her head covered with a scarf, lighting the candles, covering her eyes with her hands welcoming the Sabbath with a whispered prayer.

When Papa, Manfred and Kurt came home, Papa put his hand on his children's heads to give them a blessing, then Thea helped serve the meal, soup with matzah balls, and tender boiled chicken pieces with salad or vegetables.

My Grandma Gornitzky was devout, holding on to tradition. My Granny Weiss had no knowledge of Jewish ritual, she had been raised an atheist.

The Weiss family lived in a totally secular environment, even celebrating Christmas as a pagan festival. Eugene bought a huge Christmas tree every year on Christmas Eve, with Silent Night playing on his wind up gramophone. He carried tiny Thea blindfolded to the tree lit by a mass of flickering candles, crowned with a silver star. During the first Gornitzky/Weiss Shabbos meal together, Eugene hid in the toilet, smoking a secret cigarette. He sat thinking about the increasing threat to the Jews, in Germany. In the end it didn't matter, he thought, religious or not, our fate would be the same. He worried about Manfred's family. Would they be safe? Would they be able to make a decision to leave? They had so much to lose, their livelihood, they were no longer young. It would be difficult adapting to a new country. He worried about the young couple, they too would need his support.

"O sister! May you grow into thousands of myriads"
Genesis 24:60

Mama Gornitzky places a veil over my 19-year-old mother's head as she is about to walk down the aisle on her wedding day. It is dropped on her head without warning, to cover the divine light emanating from the bride. Her soul is considered pure and divine. Both bride and groom are closer to God during the wedding ceremony than usual. Purity needs privacy, hence the veil. Thea doesn't understand any of this. It's mid-July and boiling hot and she hates it. She had made her own simple satin dress, with a small wreath of orange blossom in her hair and now has to wear two bloody veils.

I had never understood why there were no pictures of her, did she mind?

"I wasn't bothered," she always said. "I never dreamt of being a beautiful bride, there are more important things to think about, get an education, get a profession and above all hold on to your friends. I couldn't."

They married in Berlin. Everyone was there toasting, drinking, flirting and dancing. The wedding party accompanied them to the station. Friends rushed down the platform throwing confetti at them, playing the accordion, kissing and hugging, promising to meet up.

Don't know where, don't know when;
But I know we'll meet again.

As Jews, they were forbidden to take their money out of the country, so my father spent all his cash on a six-week honeymoon journey through central Europe, the Balkans and down to Constantinople. When they caught that train to Budapest after the wedding he, aged 24, turned his back on Germany. His life in Berlin was over, his pursuit of Englishness was about to begin.

Manfred and Thea - 1937

Gornitzky family shop – Berlin c1930

Manfred and Thea's Marriage Certificate

*S*he remembered, how in the springtime, she flung nasturtium seeds everywhere and now she watched a burst of red and orange spreading over the back step, a final blaze of colour before winter.

She dances with her own shadow. It is so tall she is tempted to cut it off at her feet and keep it forever. She scrambles up the hill on all fours with the panting caramel dog. She claws the earth which crumbles in her hands and her heart thunders inside her chest. At the top they flop down, she inhales the smell of his paws, damp soil, the forest and strange animals she never sees.

Then comes the moment when the earth is floodlit by the setting sun and everything is bathed in a holy light, streaming on to the leaves, shining through translucent flowers, colours in a stained glass window. The grass is emerald. Everything is illuminated and that moment is eternity.

Still breathless from the climb, she is dazzled by the golden windows of the house across the valley. She is overcome by the urge to spread the wings folded within her. She wants to become something more than human.

Then the sky changes and the light pales.

The gold vanishes, a monochrome filter covers the trees, only the outline of the tall grass remains visible.

She descends, the dog on a lead, and sits on the step, hugging her knees. Beneath a darkening sky a sliver of cold moon emerges from behind blue mountains.

Soon Zero is plunged into darkness.

Europe is plunged into darkness.

PART TWO

War in Europe

Chapter 5

Departures and Arrivals

1939 - Departures

> ....we do not have natural continuity in our society.
> We have drastic ruptures, from one culture to
> another, over time and within a culture. That means
> people almost cease to exist at every drastic change.
> Barbara Meyerhof (Stories as equipment for Living; 2010)

After 1933 European Jews were frantic to escape the third
Reich. It was becoming difficult for them to emigrate. The Nazi
authorities created a bureaucratic maze demanding an exit
permit, a certificate of good conduct, a document confirming
taxes paid, taxes on their assets, a tax for fleeing, a passport
stamped with J (for JUDE, Jew in German), the name Moshe
added for men and Sara for women. They were only allowed a
few personal belongings and ten marks in currency.

Some countries, such as the USSR, refused entry and
others, such as the US, worked a quota limiting system. Britain
had had a legislative policy regarding immigration since the
First World War. Between 1933 and 1938 Britain attempted
to restrict the numbers of refugees whilst showing sympathy
for the plight of the Jews. Entry was permitted to those who
could bring some benefit to Britain, through the humanities,

arts and sciences, and industry. Around 70,000 refugees had arrived from Germany by 1938.

It was mainly middle class Jews living in the major cities who could afford to leave Germany; the poorer Jews, more recent arrivals from the east, lived in small towns and villages. These Jews still led a traditional life like their ancestors in the stetls of Russia and Eastern Europe. They neither had the means to escape Nazi persecution, nor were they accepted into Britain, appearing to have little to contribute to the country's wealth or well-being..

Viennese Jews suffered the most public violence and humiliation after the Anschluss when Germany marched into Austria, March 12 1938.

The Anschluss and the violent anti-Jewish pogroms known as Krystallnacht (Night of Broken Glass) caused particular devastation in Berlin and Vienna, the two largest Jewish communities in the Reich. Windows of synagogues, Jewish homes and Jewish businesses were smashed. November 9th and 10th 1938, 267 synagogues were destroyed, burning throughout the night, Jewish cemeteries were desecrated and up to 30,000 males were incarcerated on grounds of their ethnicity, first in local gaols and then transferred to Dachau Buchenwald and Sachsenhausen.

Arrivals

Thea and Manfred arrived in Leeds in September 1937. Manfred had been sick for most of their honeymoon. He was confined to his cabin with a raging fever, burning up in the realisation that he had fled his homeland and was now stateless. He was relieved to have escaped the restrictive constraints of both the orthodox rules of his religious family and also the ever tightening and dehumanising laws limiting the lives of Jewish people in Berlin.

He recognised his good fortune. He had stepped into the Weiss family, well established in England. His father-in-law would protect him financially, for a while. He lay in his cabin, determined to suppress the waves of homesickness and nausea overwhelming him on the little post boat crossing the

Bosphorus. He had no right to self–pity. He was young, in love, on the crest of a wave. So what if the Germans didn't want him? He would stop being German. Maybe this could be a seamless transition.

Working for Eugene at Longfield Mills in Heckmondwike he's no longer, a flirtatious confident young man. He has become a wary asylum seeker. He assumed the local Jewish refugee committee would support refugees, but was dismayed to read in their journal that British Jews had an ambivalent attitude to the increasing influx of Germans. Becoming aligned with 'German' nationals, albeit persecuted, Jews, threatened the British Jew's hard-earned place in British society. Here, for generations, their ethnicity had been underplayed. The German Jewish Aid committee published a pamphlet, Helpful Information and Guidance for Every Refugee, in January 1939. This warned them to avoid causing offence to the British by talking too loudly or gesturing flamboyantly and emphasised the necessity of speaking English properly and minimising their European accents. The British government were to classify these refugees as 'enemy aliens', in spite of their desire to become loyal British citizens. Later they became known as The King's Most Loyal Enemy Aliens.

In Dewsbury, Manfred could no longer pop next door to his father's perfume shop for a quick café-cognac with a pretty customer. Here, he opened his grease-proof paper packet of corned beef sandwiches and made his own mug of weak tea, sweetened with Carnation tinned milk. It was heated on a grimy gas-ring in the carbonising room. He spent much of his time at the Mill applying for visas and affidavits for extended family and friends, persuading his frail father-in-law to act as a guarantor.

To Manfred, England was the land of the free. He worked hard to speak English and embrace English traditions such as the British bobby, roast beef and Yorkshire pudding on Sundays. My father was a stranger in suburban Leeds. Those around saw him as a dark-eyed foreigner, with a strong accent, a man who loved to talk and tell jokes.

He was a married man, living in the little house that Eugene had bought for £500, keeping chickens in the backyard. He watched carefully, how his next-door neighbour,

Mr Gamble, carried coal into the house on a shovel, ready to light the fire.

"Aha," he thought, "So that's what English husbands do! I can do the same".

He learned how to twist pieces of newspaper and lay them in the grate, arrange the coal carefully in the tiled fireplace and sometimes hold a sheet of newspaper in front of the chimneybreast to encourage the flames to draw. In Berlin everyone had central heating.

More departures

After the fall of Dunkirk (26 May to 4 June 1940) and the German invasion of the Netherlands, allied confidence in winning the war was at its lowest. Fear of a potential invasion fuelled fear of spies and Nazi agents (fifth columnists). It was considered possible for spies to filter in amongst the 75,000 Jewish Austrian and German refugees who were living in the UK at that time, struggling to settle in the country.

At the time there was both strong anti-Jewish and anti-German feeling. The Churchill government came into power 11 May 1940 and Churchill issued a white paper in parliament entitled 'Collar the lot'. All male German nationals between 16 and 60 were to be interned, also female aliens were interned.

The chaotic round-ups began immediately. By mid-July 27 000 were interned, mainly in the Liverpool area. Initially many were held under canvas, in very difficult conditions, because the British government didn't know where to put them.

Manfred was in shock when he heard the radio announcement of this decree. Suddenly this young man, eager to become British, was being described by the British government as an enemy alien, he was aligned with Germans, he was a German, he could be a spy, he could damage the state. It was incomprehensible, he had been exiled by the German state, as a Jew, they had defined him as a defiling the German people. His identity made him an undesirable in both countries. When he spoke, his strong Berlin accent, branded him as the enemy so he was to be rounded up and held captive. For Thea, the quiet Leeds streets built in the early 1930s, a blue stained glass swallow on the staircase, and a tiled fireplace in the front room, was the backdrop of a calm predictable existence, despite the mayhem in Europe.

It seemed unimaginable that a bomb would drop on their home in Kingswood Gardens. These were the streets where she would wheel her babies' prams backwards and forwards to Gretchen's. This was the house where she would give birth to me. She was a newlywed, playing house, asking her mother how to turn tomatoes into soup, "where is the liquid?" She walked her little wire-haired fox terrier across the fields which stretched from Moortown all the way to Harrogate. She felt at home and forgot that she had been a Berliner She didn't yet realise that she was expecting her first English baby. She had been a child of immigrants who had chosen to take their place in a new country. She didn't fully comprehend that her husband was struggling for an identity after being forced to take his place here through persecution.

Thea and Manfred's world started spiralling out of control again, six months before Reichkristallnacht (Nov 10 1938). In May 1938 Mama, was on the phone, from Berlin, in the middle of the night. There had been a knock on the door. The Gestapo had arrested Papa, they would not wait till she had packed properly, they wouldn't let her give him any breakfast, not even a cup of coffee. She didn't know where he had been taken. He never argued, never showed them the government papers granting him permission to negotiate the move of his soap factory from Berlin to South Wales. He was afraid they would pick Kurt up too. My uncle aged nineteen was hiding in his bedroom hardly daring to breathe. What should she do? What about Kurt?

Leeds responded quickly: put Kurt on the next train over here. Loyal Leeds solicitor, Henry Hyams, also started negotiations to effect Papa's release.

Herman and Edith Gornitzky

Mama buys Kurt a return rail ticket Berlin-Leeds. Half an hour before the train reaches the Dutch border the German border police walk along the train. Kurt is nineteen and he is frightened. He is alone, travelling to England for the first time. He does not speak English. He has left his mother in the flat and his father has been taken away. He sits shaking on the train. It stops at the Dutch border, the German customs official, looks at him, a forged passport without the J for Jude printed on it, acquired by Papa, preparing for emigration . Something is not right. He looks into my uncle's dark eyes, recognising immediately that he is Jewish. He looks back at the passport.

The train is halted and waits for instructions from Berlin headquarters. Whilst they are waiting Kurt suddenly pulls his ticket out.

"I am going to visit my brother in Leeds," he says, "for a holiday. I am coming back in three weeks."

They examine his return ticket, nod briefly, hand back his passport and wave the train through to Holland. Kurt never returned.

Papa meanwhile was incarcerated in Buchenwald concentration camp for six weeks where he met his brother Semmi. He had thought he had been protected through his false papers and correspondence with the German government, papers where he had even written Sieg Heil underneath his signature..

Leeds were desperate for Mama and Papa to board the train to England on his release; but Mama wouldn't move until she had nursed him back to health, describing him as a 'broken man', mentally and physically. He had been starved.

Later my cousin Ronnie asked him what the worst of that experience was.

He simply answered: "The dogs."

He never saw Semmi again.

At last all the Gornitzkys were safe, squashed into Thea and Manfred's little house. The men sat reading the papers, pairs of large feet in front of the fire. Mama commandeered the tiny kitchen whilst Scamp shivered on the back doorstep in the cold.

More arrivals

My grandparents Weiss household was also expanding. Gretchen's brother, George, and his wife Beattie arrived from Berlin, penniless. Beattie shuffled round her kitchen floor, cleaning the lino with two large cloths wrapped round her feet. They lived in my grandmother's dining room until the end of the war, eventually renting a small flat in Chapeltown. This had always been the area of new immigrants, Jews escaping pogroms from Poland and Russia at the turn of the previous century, then the Irish during the potato famine, later the Afro–Caribbean community arriving in the 1950s on the 'Windrush'. My brother and I visited them after school, on a red tram that shook, rattled and rolled. Toby dog ambling along, attached to us by a length of skipping rope. We were eager to play with the few objects from Berlin on their mantelpiece. These included an orchestra comprised of bronze cats, each playing a different instrument and a box with a lapis lazuli songbird that popped out and warbled when the lid jumped open.

We squashed up to them in their cramped living room filled with my grandmother's giant sideboard, carved with cherubs holding grapes in dark wood. We were telling them stories in German (they had little English) about the hated sago pudding every Tuesday for school dinners. We showed them how we taught Toby to sit on command. Johnny sang *All Things Bright and Beautiful,* and I recited *You are old father William.* We ate biscuits, drank our milk and hugged them before chasing each other down the street to the tram stop. Their experience of England was through our stories. Their own grandson, Harry, grew up far away in Chile.

Uncle George conducted a small business from the flat in Chapeltown. He wrote careful letters to his customers, assisted by an English dictionary. He never wanted to meet the customers face-to-face. He feared they would mistrust him when they heard his German accent, find him too old and take their business elsewhere.

I understood later that George saved his pennies for Harry. During the 1950s they received restitution payments. This was money paid out by the governments of Germany and Austria as compensation for victims murdered and persecuted by Nazi Germany and Austria. As well as payments for murdered relatives, compensation was paid for lost housing, destroyed businesses, liquidated bank accounts, loss of education and opportunity.

At a conference between West Germany and Israel in 1951, Adenauer, then German chancellor, stated that unspeakable crimes had been committed in the name of the German people which called for moral and material indemnity. David Ben-Gurion, then president of Israel, believed this might help towards a spiritual settlement of infinite suffering. As a consequence by the 1960s the financial situation for many of the Jewish refugees had changed considerably.

Harry from Chile eventually visited Leeds. I sat on my own grandmother's knee watching this tall young man embrace his grandparents, none of them speaking a common language. There were tears, laughter and much cake eating. I helped my mother light the Shabbos candles; the wine and bread was blessed in the few words of Hebrew we could all recite together.

Frieda, Gretchen's youngest sister arrived in England late at night, by train, no English. She smuggled in a birdcage, covered with a thick dark cloth, desperate that Moppy, her canary, would sleep through the journey believing it was just another dark night in the Berlin apartment. He did sleep through that night living out his destiny to lift her beyond her loneliness and be loved by us post-war children. When he died in Leeds, my brother and I bought her a new canary with our pocket money. We all watched Mitzi sing of Leeds in the new life. Moppy had sung of Berlin and the old life.

Frieda had learnt how to make chocolates at the ORT school, the Jewish training centre, offering free training to Jews about to flee Nazism, during her final weeks in Berlin. People waiting anxiously for entry visas to far-flung countries learnt a new trade, not dependant on language, to be able to earn a living. My great aunt had chosen to ease her path with homemade chocolates. She never sold any but took over my grandmother's kitchen in the week before Hanukah when the sweet smell of melting chocolate filled the house. We weren't allowed to peep round the kitchen door so waited in eager anticipation until we exchanged presents after my father had lit the candles. She made cardboard boxes, tied with coloured ribbons and inside, nestling in fine tissue, were six small exquisitely shaped chocolates. They were diamonds, teddies, daisies, angels. Every one had a different flavour - crème truffle, marzipan, hazelnut, each with its own unique decoration on top, a tiny piece of angelica cut like a flower, a circlet of silver dragees, a delicate tiny heart painted with edible gold leaf.

She was always sad that we ate them quickly. She beseeched us (in German) to savour the flavour, to eat them slowly, to appreciate the work that went into them. Maybe my brother and I tossed those boxes aside carelessly. I remembered them after she died, when I thought more about her story. I wondered how it was to sit on the train clutching Moppy, escaping on a dark winter's night, with chocolate recipes in her head but no money and no English.

Lucy was the eldest sister. Her son had already emigrated to Israel (then Palestine) and she was to join him there when her visa came through. Meanwhile, she shared Frieda's bedroom and together they would pour over the modern Hebrew alphabet printed large in a child's reading primer. She asked her youngest sister how she would do her shopping. She was worried she wouldn't be able to read labels in the shops. The siblings never saw each other again. Flying to Israel was too expensive and they were all reluctant to uproot, even for a few weeks or months. They wanted to stay where they were. They wanted nothing out of routine to happen. They wanted to feel safe.

Lucy sent letters from Israel describing the dusty town of Ramat Hasharon, their cramped flat, the terrible heat. She sent pictures of her two grandchildren in white shorts squinting at the camera in bright sunlight. She missed the cold in Berlin and the times they all went ice-skating together, wearing furry hats and muffs.

I asked my Mum if she was nice. She sat quietly for what seemed a long time. Then turned to me and answered,

"She lived in NeuKoln. We went there every Shabbos by tram."

Calman Sisters

1940

Mama, Papa and my uncle Kurt settle in Northumberland Street, Salford. None of them speak much English yet. My father's family is struggling to survive. They feel indebted to Eugene Weiss's support but now it's time to stand on their own feet. They worry about the family left behind. They never talk about them; a silence fills the empty spaces of their thoughts and fears. They buy vegetable oil, and start making kosher potato crisps. The crisps are selling but as soon as the government rations vegetable oil, it's over. They lose money investing in a fryer and tins; they need cash and decide to manufacture kosher soap.

My grandfather, by chance, met his Rabbi from the well-established Munchenerstrasse synagogue in Berlin. They were suddenly face-to-face on the street in Manchester, embracing each other, hardly able to believe their eyes. The rabbi supported the Gornitzky soap business and so they were able to sell to Jewish retail outlets in the area.

My uncle meets a lovely Jewish girl from Hamburg at the cinema, my Aunty Helga. They get engaged. The May blossom was just dusting the trees with tiny white and pink flowers. Everything is coming to life again. Then a knock at the door in the middle of the night, just as it happened before in the Berlin flat on the Kantstrasse. Again a knock. They open the door; uniformed officers stand there with an arrest warrant.

There is a loud crash my uncle has fainted with fear, over six foot of him flat out on the kitchen floor. Mama packs their holdall whilst they quickly eat some breakfast. They are being interned by the British government.

Mama phones Leeds. Manfred has also been picked up. He has spent the night in the cells at Leeds town hall. They were all herded onto an overcrowded train in sweltering heat with no food or drink, bound for Huyton transit camp, Liverpool, at the height of the Liverpool blitz. The three men are pleased to be together.

They were fetched, in the middle of the night. .

There was a knock on the door at one in the morning.

That phrase often ran through my mind. I often dreamt about European Jews safely tucked up in bed, soft pillows, warm central-heated rooms, snoring quietly until a rat-tat-tat on the door tore them out of sleep. Then my dream would always turn to the sound of the trains.

I am now a grey-haired English woman, walking my dog through the vineyards of Alsace. I tend my garden, the purple allium heads, the fruit trees, branches heavy with ripe red plums, a mass of golden sunflowers. But my monochrome dream of cattle-trucks speeding over tracks on their way to the East is still an unwelcome visitor in the night, forever rattling to oblivion at the end of the line.

The three Gornitzky men, Herman, the father, Kurt and Manfred, the sons, appeared before a hastily assembled tribunal to confirm their classification. There were three classification categories for enemy aliens. They assumed they were in Class C, a refugee from Nazi oppression and of no danger to the state. Each case had been decided, sometimes very arbitrarily, by the particular judge in the individual tribunal.

Thea meanwhile moved into her parents' house, to help her mother manage the household of eight people. She reluctantly re-homed Scamp and again settled into a life not chosen but dictated by circumstance.

2010

At my mother's cremation, as the last Jew in the Leeds family I recite Kaddish (the Jewish prayer for the dead which gives thanks for the life just ended). I sound like a five year old as I struggle with the Aramaic words.

She had talked more about Berlin in her last weeks than ever before, so where was home for her? Indeed, for both my parents, I ask myself staring at the plain plywood coffin. Berlin or Yorkshire? The curtains closed and the coffin creaked into oblivion. Marlene Dietrich's voice sang the German lyrics to I still have a suitcase in Berlin.

Ich hab' noch einen Koffer in Berlin
Deswegen muss ich nächstens wieder hin.
Die Seligkeiten vergang'ner Zeiten
Sind alle noch in meinem kleinen Koffer drin.

I still have a suitcase in Berlin
That's why I have to go there sometime soon.
The joys of days gone by
Are all still in my little suitcase.

I remember the letters, correspondence from when Manfred was interned, time when my parents were no longer there but not yet here. They were in a paper packet, two bundles of letters tied with brown string.

1940 – Huyton

The three men arrive in Huyton which was a half-built housing estate constructed by Liverpool Corporation. The boundary of the camp was an eight-metre high barbed wire fence. Searchlights were erected over the fence illuminating the high wooden shooting platforms.

The Gornitzkys must have been amongst the first men to arrive. They were transported to Huyton in mid-June. By July 1940 around 5 000 men were accommodated there. They were not allowed to send or receive any mail for a number of weeks after arriving at the camp. They received no news of the war and did not know if their own families were safe. As they arrived, Liverpool was suffering heavy bomb raids. The worst attacks were in May 1941 by over 600 German planes. Nearly 2,000 Liverpool people were killed in one week alone and many more left homeless and injured.

There are conflicting reports about the British administration's attitudes to internees. Manfred spoke English by the time he was interned so was 'given a job' helping Major Thomas in his office translating letters and processing requests for releases or affidavits. The English officer and German Jew worked well together, they shared personal information,

Thomas had his wedding anniversary and I put him a couple of flowers on his table. He sends you good wishes. He has never spent a wedding day at home yet, always called away (letter from Manfred to Thea)

Six thousand internees were shipped to Australia and Canada. Manfred was eager to apply for a passage to Canada, on a ship due to leave. He visualised a civilian ship travelling alongside imagining him and Thea holding hands as they travelled together to the New World. Thea, blocking out her European roots and German identity, was adamant she belonged in Leeds. The Arandora Star left Liverpool on 2nd July 1940 without him, carrying 1,216 German, mainly Jewish, and Italian internees. It was struck by a German torpedo off the coast of Ireland and only 586 survived.

The British public was shocked by this and, as a consequence, began to be more sympathetic towards the refugees. By late summer the Government produced a white paper that slowly triggered the release process of internees, although the randomness and inefficiency of this process meant that in spite of tirelessly fighting bureaucracy Manfred had to wait another nine months before he was freed.

Chapter 6

Internment

2012

I'm looking at two piles of brown flimsy envelopes, one hundred and four letters, my parents' correspondence between May 1940 and January 1941. An account of their rite of passage into adulthood, a father's death, a son's birth, internment, tussling with bureaucracy, stormy seas and parcels of washing, parcels of food, parcels of birthday presents, parcels with a hundred lovely things.

I can't decipher their handwriting. Their correspondence is in illegible German script which renders them inaccessible, unlike my memory of the shouting, whispering, warning and comforting sound of their German voices.

***

I'm bumping along in the back seat behind Claude the fire chief from Alsace and his partner, Claudine. The blue mountains of the Vosges are behind us. We are in the valley heading for the Black Forest ahead. It's hard to tell when it changes from France to Germany.

I am living in Alsace, because one day, still wearing silver earrings - now with matching silver hair - I fell in love with an English man who fell in love with France on a school trip at the age of fourteen. He learnt French by listening to the radio and reading French newspapers. Many years later he worked in the European Parliament, driving every month between Strasbourg and Bruxelles, a parliament symbolic of European unity. He took me home to Europe, driving between Alsace and London. Sometimes I walk our spaniel on Hampstead Heath, sometimes deep in the foothills of the Vosges The man from the European Parliament is on his hands and knees blocking mouse holes in the kitchen, and we eat cheese on toast for tea in front of his European *Kacheloffen,* the traditional tiled, wood burning fire. Half our lives are in French, half in English.

I tell Claude about the letters. He is an Alsatian, his family had been French then they had been German now they were French again. They had been forced to change their nationality according to the country that occupied them. He understood how when speaking a different language, one becomes a different person. His mother had been evacuated at the age of twelve to south-west France and when she returned Alsace had been colonised by the Germans: German street signs, German first language in school, German names for the children. She never spoke about it. She just described the food in south-west France, different from Alsace. She simply said "It was like a holiday".

Claude: an interest in words and language is part of my roots - my parents were in Strasbourg during a five-year occupation, in a German school. It's part of their life and so it's part of mine.

His mother had never mentioned what she faced when getting off the train in Strasbourg station - the rows of flags with swastikas, the German soldiers.

Claude told me about one of his heroes, Jean-François Champollion, the French classical scholar who deciphered Egyptian hieroglyphics in the 19th century. He is about to appoint himself as the bridge between my parents' voices and my understanding. Claude becomes the Champollion of the Gornitzky correspondence.

He drives a bright red van. He has an irresistible chuckle, a large moustache, and shrugging shoulders. He chops his vegetables very small – never tomatoes, never beetroot, never carrots. I always wonder whether his aversion to red fruit and vegetables has to do with fighting red and orange flames in his youth.

Claudine wears red dresses, zigzagged striped or dotted with orange. She gardens in red-suede, ribboned shoes, and a cigarette dangling from her mouth.

I walk my dog down a twisting lane leading to the forest full of deer and wild boar. We pass white horses in the field and I pause on the bridge to throw sticks into the stream for Sammy to fetch. Smoke curls out of the cottage chimney where the woodcutter lives, the pine trees outside make his two rooms dark and cold. Sometimes his little white dog 'Appy, with pointed ears and a curly tail, picks his way down the path to say hello with a gentle wag of the tail, a lick on the hand and a sniff of Sammy's rear. The woodcutter told me proudly, "'Appy is an English name."

"'Appy?" I was puzzled; he nodded proudly. "Ah," I realised, "you mean 'Appy, like 'appy birthday."

Goldfinches are searching for berries ripening on the hedgerows and we turn by a grassy bank. Claude's goats are tethered on the hillside bleating in tune with their bells as they chew the grass.

Claude and Claudine live in a house with blue shutters. I pass the incongruous new build, on the corner with its manicured lawn out of bounds to 'Appy. Petruschka is at the window, watering neat red geraniums with her blonde hair piled up away from her beautiful, wide-boned, Russian face. I wave a greeting and stroke her Pomeranian crossbreed, a small moth-eaten creature, on its last legs, named Tolstoy.

Once I have passed the china blue hydrangeas Claude is within reach. I am delivering the two new letters. "Le facteur arrive." I hand over the small envelopes, stamped 'Opened BY CENSOR', two at a time. Claude e-mails the transcription, I translate.

Here he describes what led to his involvement with this correspondence:

> *In the letters I find a different perspective to the history of the Second World War - my uncle crossed over to London. I didn't know there were*

internment camps here. I was curious therefore transcribed the letters. I had the opportunity to enter into the 'intime' part of the life of two persons. European foreign parents of my friend, which were not completely strange to me.

My parents, as they were long ago, found their way into Claude's life. His curiosity about their lives enabled him to decipher their script, smile at their jokes, worry about their baby and wait anxiously for news from the Home Office. He studied my parents' handwriting. He asked me questions about their relationship, their food, their friends, their hopes, and fears. He wanted to know my 24-year-old parents intimately so that he could replace undecipherable words with a guess from the sense he gleaned of the paragraph and the feeling in his heart.

I enter completely in the other person at that moment - what did he want to say?

Our combined encounter with the past lasted a whole summer during which he deciphered and I translated 105 letters from German into English. Claude and I engaged in a dialogue about the content and meaning within the letters.

I know things about this family, those normally no-one talks about. It is an enrichment in our (Carry and me) relationship.

I have woven fragments of our conversations around the text of the letters.

Internment

The sacred is in the ordinary...it is to be found in one's daily life, in one's neighbours, friends, and family, in one's own backyard...
Abraham Maslow

The army issued tuck-in letter sheets. These were made of chemically prepared paper to expose invisible ink. Internees were only allowed to write twenty-four lines, four hundred and twenty words, which initially Manfred found difficult.

"So, Darling, the 24 lines-are done, for today's exchange, only room left for a thousand kisses for you and baby. Please come and see me."

Both sides of the correspondence were opened by the censor. Claude and I remarked how their letters were composed of trivial details of their lives. We wondered whether this was an expression of intimacy or whether the content was constrained by the censor.

> *Claude: What's not said might be the most important things that are happening.*

My parents described how they experienced their rite of passage into adulthood differently through their letters between May 1940 and January 1941.

> *Claude: He is interned nine months; her pregnancy begins at the beginning of internment. She is speaking to a man she calls 'mein Junge' (my boy). It's my feeling that he's the second baby. She is two times pregnant. She takes care of this man nine months long and after he becomes free.*

Manfred had embraced a new identity as a continental Brit with hope and optimism, the gradually increasing shame and humiliation he had experienced as a Jew in Berlin was receding. Becoming an enemy alien was a painful echo of the dehumanising effect of the Nuremberg laws. His new identity was slipping away from him. He was now simply a Jew behind barbed wire.

Thea, meanwhile, was supporting her parents. Her father was dying and her mother was managing a household full of penniless siblings adjusting to new lives as refugees. .

Claude and I became curious about what was being omitted from the letters. We were both scrutinising the text for hints about their states of mind, stories of the war, the fate of family members left behind in Germany, the effects of trauma.

I attempted to fill this gap by researching the internment and reading passages to Claude. My books are in English, I read aloud to him and we translated into French together as we went along and so gleaned a more comprehensive picture of life in the camp as well as government policy.

The first stage of Manfred's internment was spent in Huyton. He was with his father and brother. His early letters are focused on obtaining a release for his father.

He writes to Thea:

Manfred (M): *Many thanks for making the application for me. Let us hope for a good result. The only chance to get my father out of here is on account of his illness. I arranged today that he was examined by the medical officer who has already sent his report to the Home Office saying he is unfit for internment.*

What he doesn't tell her is that there were ten men living in a small house designed for a family of four; that it was only because of Papa's age that they had not been assigned to a tent. Their washing and toilet facilities were minimal.

M: *There are many lectures here in the camp, Papa has just returned from one about Goethe; he says it's the first opportunity he has ever found for education.*

By the next letter his father is released.

M: *Hello darling, Papa's release came through and we just sent the old man off. We went with him in the luggage lorry to the station in Liverpool and waved him goodbye, under escort of course. At present, we are working like hell. Major Thomas is in charge of the releases, so you can imagine how busy we are. We are sending all the old and sick people home.*

Kurt and Manfred remained behind, believing that their own release would be imminent. Manfred constantly seeks approval from the British administration. He wanted to obey rules thus demonstrating his loyalty to the British and hopefully speeding up his release.

M: *Please don't include any newspapers or letters in my parcels as this is strictly forbidden, but you can send letters separately and without stamps as they are internee mail and therefore free of charge. No newspapers - in case we are Jerry!*

The relationship with the Home Office was a lifeline for all internees. Jewish refugees were interned alongside Nazi sympathisers.

M: *Simply write to the Home Office over and over again. Don't let up writing in English, to prove we are not spies.*

Every letter from Manfred is desperately asking for a visit.

M: *Have you heard anything in connection with the visiting permit? Now the HO organises their own admin, we have daily visitors, they say they have obtained permits without difficulties. So let me hope.......*

What Manfred is not telling her is that on his arrival he was issued with a sack that he filled with straw to use as a paillasse.

When Thea visited Huyton she was instructed to walk round the perimeter of the camp straight into the office. By taking this route she didn't see the waterlogged and muddy streets between the houses. She was unaware of the tents where some of the men slept and all of them ate. Manfred led her to believe the situation was better than its reality. Later she used to describe walking around the barbed wire fence, past the watchtowers looking for the entrance, when she visited. She sat in the office, which belonged to the camp superintendent, Captain Thomas. Manfred's work for British administration gave him a warm, quiet place to entertain her.

Thea's response to the visit:

Thea (T): *Yesterday I had a good sleep, it was after all a bit stressful. I hadn't realised it's like a prison there... I got a lift from a young girl to Liverpool Lime Street station, which was really comfortable; as a result I had time for a snack at the station refreshment room. It was already 10.20 when I arrived back in Leeds. Harry fetched me and my parents were here at our house to hear all your news. I would love to come all the time, I can't believe the difference it makes if I have seen you and spoken to you, I feel I can carry on for a while. Now, my love I am more with you in my thoughts than in Leeds.*

His longing for home showed through in the letter following one of her visits:

M: *Now you are again in Leeds and I am still here. But anyhow I was so happy to see you for a few hours and I feel much better now. And I think you are more satisfied too... Darling, I feel to thank you for all that which you are doing for me now, especially with the baby coming. And please don't give up, as I now realise what freedom means.*

Two days ago you were here and it'll be high time you come again. Bring cake again so we can have café together, last time everyone left us alone at the table even though it was the office. We'll work that out again for next time.

Clinging to the ritual of coffee and cake, a reminder of how things once were in Germany. He longed for the old *Gemutlichkeit* (cosiness) of his previous existence. What happens when all the little rituals and ways of being that have been taken for granted disappear?

He fears he is becoming invisible and searches for ways of reminding the outside world he still exists.

M: *I have the feeling a number of birthdays will have passed. Perhaps you could write the dates, so I can send congratulations.*

He longs to see the family all in one room, oblivious of how unwell his father-in-law has become, and the impossibility of getting Mama and Papa to Huyton.

M: *Listen all of you, why don't you come here together. I'll send a telegram whether Tuesday and Saturday would work, if we can get a permit. You could of course come any day; the visiting days are Tuesday and Saturday. Then come always around 2 so you can stay the whole afternoon, on visiting days even up to 5.30pm. Million kisses.*

They're both constantly frustrated by the irregularity of the post.

M: *I wait with longing for the post, please write very often. By the way you do not need to frank the letters, but you have to write on the envelope Internee mail free of charge. Give everyone lots of love*

She writes:

T: *Darling the last letter I had was dated ten days ago, I'm expecting some post from you daily and it doesn't arrive. Weber regularly receives twice weekly letters from Fred....I've not had a letter from you for a whole week now. How is that? Have you got so many other girls to write to?*

He never told her that initially there was not enough to eat. The men took turns in cooking meals for groups of thirty men. One internee remarked: *What was a pinch of salt for a family, became a handful of salt when cooking in the camp.*

Accounts and diaries revealed that portions were the equivalent of three spoonfuls of food per day; porridge, with no sugar, and two slices of bread for breakfast, vegetable stew with potatoes for lunch, bread and cheese, tea and a little jam for high tea.

He has not been explicit about the eating conditions, the sitting in long rows out of doors peeling potatoes. He begs Thea to provide an electric plate so he can cook for himself.

M: *Even electric articles are now officially allowed. Herr Lorant has already had his cooker since fourteen days; and I have nothing to make myself something warm in the evenings at home. Many have requested hotplates, they're very practical. We have 230 volts AC.*

Her reply:

T: *Mother has an electric plate she has bequeathed to us! Harry has taken it to Crossland electricians to test if it's OK and I will send it tomorrow.*

He pressurises but still doesn't let her know that there is not sufficient food.

M: *I am really annoyed; everyone in the camp has comfort except me. I can't even heat up the smallest thing; I don't believe they're unavailable. I'm not asking for too much. This has gone on for six weeks that I'm begging for it.*

She replies:

T: *Mother's boiling plate was dangerous so I had to run through the whole town, finally one shop ordered one, it'll be delivered so I'll send it tomorrow and pack a few things in with it.*

At last it arrives.

M: *Many thanks for the plate. It is quite practical and efficient. It also shows that you have understood what I need. Above all send me some continental bread.*

As soon as the plate arrives the endless requests for food begins and will continue to the end of the internment.

M: *I could do with some jam and compote, cold meats, corned beef lobster etc., whatever is available. The taste of the chicken still lingers on my tongue!*

M: *The best is the electric cooker. The chicken lasted three meals. Yesterday I used the fat to fry up part of the onion with potatoes, it was unbelievable. Millions of kisses.*

Two days later:

M: *Now I'm really cross, since your last visit I just got two letters and no parcel. How come? You can send everything you want except cigarettes*

She replies:

T: *Quickly a couple of lines, so that you hear from me, a parcel is being sent in the same post. I think I'm very prompt at fulfilling your wishes. It's often not easy to get hold of everything these days....I can't find your braces.*

His reply:

M: *Chocolate cake I got, otherwise I have received nothing. You need to get organised, my mother sent me cold lambs tongues yesterday, and it arrived safely and was a feast.*

She calmly responds without rising to the bait:

T: *I just sent two parcels, your washing, jam, fruit and the tongue which I pickled last week! Nice? I'm as pleased when I send them as when I eat them myself.*

And later:

M: *Mama sends fortnightly packages which were delivered within two days. From you I have no parcel and only one letter in three weeks.*

She writes:

T: *Your child says Hi. He just gave me a big kick for emphasis. Many kisses.*

> Claude: *At first I didn't like the father, reading his letters. Then Carry gave me her mother's letters, completely different - a life philosophy. At the same time the father became more 'sympathetica', I saw both sides, one fed into the other. Her side showed him differently.*

Now he's desperate again about the visiting permit.

M: *I got your telegram about the visiting permit. It should arrive any day. I hope I will have seen you before this letter arrive.*

Her reply:

T: *My new application for a visit permit is on the way. I hope for an early reply. But I know people who have waited for weeks.*

> *Hopefully you will have received two parcels from me, shoes, flannel trousers and chocolate. One with plimsolls, coffee, one soup, one tin of salmon, one cheese and Harry put tobacco in*
>
> *I am homesick for you again. In the end I only think about my next visit, my regards to the officers I met*

They are both frustrated by the lack of continuity in their correspondence and must adjust to the lack of control over lives forced to run in parallel, distant from each other. Thea is worried about her father's deteriorating health. Manfred is responding to captivity with increased desperation. The inmates of Huyton transit camp are constantly exposed to the night time air raids of the Liverpool blitz. He never let Thea know that the bombing had been so severe.

If this second country would let him down where would he end up? Would he disappear like his friends disappeared?

He writes about air raids;

M: *Did you have any air raids recently? Here everything is alright. The Jerries came a few times but were chased off by our fighters and anti-aircraft guns without doing any damage.*

M: *How are the air raids doing? Here it is wonderfully quiet.*

M: *We just had a little air raid. The AA (Anti-Aircraft) shoots quite well, and I imagine how you and baby sit in the shelter.*

After his father's release Manfred tries to settle. He is sustained by the routine of the office work and the support of Major Thomas. He attempts to organise his domestic and working life.

He writes:

M: *It is Sunday après-midi; I am in the office to finish today's work. Capt. Thomas is in Southport this afternoon, he works very hard indeed*

M: *My flat is now very cosy; I just need a table cloth. Then you could move in.*

Their lives will eventually intertwine again.

September 1940

Eugene's funeral and Manfred's transfer to the Isle of Man

Thea is watching her father's coffin being lowered into the grave. This is an orthodox burial for a secular man. She is standing in the United Hebrew cemetery. Trans Pennine trains rush past, from Leeds to Manchester and back again, drowning the thud of earth falling on the coffin lid. There are footsteps on the gravel and she looks up and sees Manfred approaching, between two police officers. He fumbles with his handcuffs to remove his leather shoes and stands in his socks at his father-in law's grave, the only family member who knows how to recite the Kaddish. He was granted a special permit to attend. His guards hold his siddur (prayer book) open for him. Thea had made him lunch in the hope that he would be allowed to attend. After the short ceremony they kiss briefly at the gates of the cemetery and she gives him a packet wrapped in greaseproof paper, a piece of chicken with fried onions.

He returns immediately and is preoccupied with the approaching Rosh Hashana (Jewish New Year), anxious to arrive back in Liverpool by sundown. There he is greeted with the news of his transfer to the Isle of Man, used for prisoners of war in the First World War and now to become home to Britain's fifteen thousand enemy aliens.

His first priority is to decide in which Jewish community he will say his Rosh Hashanah prayers. Although he had in recent years been leaning towards the reform movement, tonight he felt the need to hear the familiar orthodox liturgy of his childhood.

M: *My dearest dumpling. Now I am here again and in two hours is Rosh Hashana. I am going to the orthodox Jews tonight. We arrived in Liverpool an hour late, drank a beer there and were home at 5pm, I was completely done in. It was all a bit much for me at once, No air-raid. So dumpling, all the very best and hugs. Many kisses to Gretchen. Shana Tova! (Happy New Year)*

He then comments on the funeral and gives her the news of his transfer.

M: *I was so pleased I could be there. How did it all go? Did Gretchen calm down? She needs to recover totally. Monday a transport goes to the Isle of Man,*

M: *I don't need much, so leave everything where it is. I will need a change of clothes, the camp will be smaller, but that's not so bad.*

He doesn't realise that he will not see Thea until his release, many months later.

She does realise, when she receives this news. It is the moment when Thea's baby reached its tiny hand out to her and whispered "you'll have to do it alone". She supports her mother, reorganises her life and focuses on her coming baby. Manfred's life meanwhile is like a fragile mobile, hanging by a thread. He feels everything is out of balance. Death (losing his dependable father-in-law, Eugene) and birth (waiting for the new baby) stand side by side. They mirror the loss of his friends in Germany and his re birth and reinvention of his life in England. He must now undergo another move as a prisoner, another dangerous boat journey, with German U-boats lurking in the Irish Sea. He is struggling with his own chaos, a little vessel tossed by huge waves in a stormy sea.

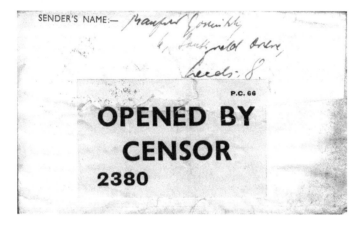

Censored letter

A.R.10.

Any communication on the subject of this letter should be addressed to :—

THE UNDER SECRETARY OF STATE,
HOME OFFICE
(ALIENS DEPARTMENT),
P.O. BOX No. 100,
PADDINGTON DISTRICT OFFICE,
LONDON, W.2.

and the following number quoted :—

G7223/7

HOME OFFICE,

P.O. BOX No. 100,

PADDINGTON
DISTRICT OFFICE,

P.O. BOX No. 2. LONDON, W.2.

BOURNEMOUTH,
16th December, 1940.
HANTS.

The Under Secretary of State has

to refer to the letter dated **23rd ultimo**

regarding **Manfred Gornitzky.**

The matter is under consideration

and a decision will be communicated

as soon as possible. **A Medical Report**

has been called for.

Mrs. T. Gornitzky,
24 Kingswood Garden,
Leeds, 8.

Letter from Home Office – December 1940

Claude Dollinger – Sketching, Douglas Promenade

Sefton Hotel, Isle of Man

Isle of Man

There were several camps scattered around the Isle of Man, housing about five thousand people during the height of internment. The camps in Douglas, on the promenade, had been boarding houses and small hotels, the owners had been forced to leave their homes at short notice as the army requisitioned them for enemy aliens, mainly Jews and Italians and some Nazi sympathisers.

The Isle of Man, capital Douglas, is a self-governing British Crown Dependency, located in the Irish Sea between Great Britain and Ireland, its foreign relations and defence are the responsibility of the British Government. The British monarch holds the title of Lord of Mann and is represented by a Lieutenant Governor.

There were six camps for male internees in Douglas. The Sefton Hotel was the smallest, holding six hundred men. Older internees were placed there because there was a lift. Manfred shared an attic room, facing east overlooking the sea, with two other men. It was an improvement after the room in Huyton. The female internees were housed in the south of the Island in Port St Mary and Port Erin.

Generally the internees accepted their situation, respected the English, and were pleased to be safely out of mainland Europe. Each camp created its own activities, artistic and cultural life. Many offered English lessons. Émigrés were encouraged to take classes so that they would lose their German accents and eventually speak 'educated' English. Camp newspapers were printed in a mixture of German and English to demonstrate their life and commitment to English. There were many eminent academics in the camp, young internees who were eager to continue their education attended the lectures on offer. A square surrounded by houses formed Hutchinson Camp. It was situated on a hill behind the promenade and provided accommodation to most of the resident artists. The square was used for open-air musical concerts.

Manfred puts on a brave face. The sea journey, in glorious weather does not seem threatening and calms him. This is reflected in his description of the arrival on Isle of Man.

M: *So we arrived here safely, I sent you a telegram immediately. The crossing was beautiful. Bright sunshine and very jolly; your old man at the helm. I'm again in the office; very kind officers. Our accommodation, in the middle of Douglas, is very nice. Right on the front, it must be lovely in summer. I'm sorry now that we weren't moved earlier and you could have visited here during the fine weather. The air is very clear. Above all no air raids. Our departure from Huyton was magnificent.*

Will you send me a parcel soon? With 100 lovely things- it's such a pleasure when one gets something from home.

The food parcels from Leeds become the only certainty; they are proof of the love waiting for him. How to prepare the food and with whom to eat is his main preoccupation, indeed the only place where he can take charge.

He jokes about his accommodation - the image created by living in a hotel heading his letters from *Sefton Hotel De Luxe*.

For a while Manfred's mood lifts and his letters are more buoyant, although historical accounts suggest that food was scarce, as at Huyton. Weather becomes a metaphor of Manfred's emotional state during the remaining two months of his internment.

M: *The weather is wonderful, like summer. Douglas position is quite fantastic. In a bay and looks like Nice (in the south of France). Even the sea is blue. My office is on the promenade with a direct view, through barbed wire. If only I was free to stroll there*

M: *Yesterday your packet arrived with the potatoes and a jar of schmaltz. It came just in time for Shabbos. I now always eat with Koenig in my room, it's more pleasant than the dining area. So I really smeared a lot of gravy with schmaltz made with water and onion and fried potatoes with it; to finish, a cup of coffee with your chocolate cake. Yes, love after all passes partly through the stomach.*

This is the first time he mentions friends/room-mates. Soon he is watching the friends around him getting their releases with mounting frustration.

M: *Koenig will now be home, the HO has recommended his release; he just has to go to the advisory committee. Lorant is a good man and got Fuchs out and now Koenig,*

Meanwhile Thea is becoming increasingly involved in her baby and this vision of the future is sustaining her.

> *Claude says: Carry's mother was pregnant - that*
> *is the story within the story. Mother is completely*
> *in the pregnancy and tries to pull her husband*
> *into it.*

T: *Beloved boy.........Tomorrow I am going to see the doctor again. But judging by the kicking it must be a little Manfred or a little devil; it feels like a revolution in my tummy sometimes ...*

This afternoon I am going with Gretchen to start buying baby things, at least some cheap knitting wool at the market.

My love, what's going on inside me I don't have to describe to you? I feel so well, with it all. And you know, not everything you read and hear is correct, how a woman experiences all her thoughts as she is about to become a mother. I am so pleased and content with it

> *Claude observes: You have the feeling the father*
> *is interested but not completely - he has another*
> *preoccupation. Wants to be near but is in fact*
> *in another situation. Between the words on the*
> *page I feel Manfred is overpowered by his sense*
> *of loss and loneliness.*

Manfred answers:

M: *Has baby made any sounds? Tears are pouring down my cheeks as I write this. I must sometimes feel low; it would be much better if you could visit regularly. Kisses*

> *Claude: She reassures him. I notice in their*
> *correspondence that he has also become more*
> *like her child, needing encouragement.*

T: *My beloved boy...we are doing everything possible to bring you home...*

T: *We must keep telling each other to keep our spirits up, don't let things get us down. Everything will change again*

His frustration increases. This makes him increase the pressure for the family to lobby the Home Office.

M: *Simply write to the Home Office, whether they will do a medical examination. I don't want that my case shall stay* behind as less important. On the contrary it belongs into the front line. Please show everybody concerned my letters as I can't write to everybody. Well that is that. But believe me, Darling, I am not desperate and I don't lose my nerves.

She writes back:

T: *Write to the solicitor yourself tell them about your release ideas and what should be done. I'll try this week to speak to Milner. Otherwise I don't know what else to do. I'm just as flummoxed as you. I daren't be too down and must have patience. We'll try hardship again. Everything takes months...*

He turns his attention to food again.

M: *Send me some jam. The last was fantastic, you know my taste.*

M: *Unfortunately the jam jar broke in the parcel and I'm just clearing it up; pity, home grown strawberries.*

He grew the strawberries in their little back garden, next to the vegetable patch he'd dug after watching how his neighbour had carefully planted potatoes, leeks, carrots and tomatoes. He'd mulched the strawberries with the chicken droppings. They had been keeping chickens too. He had helped Thea and her mother stir the strawberries and sugar into a bubbling syrupy mush. It was then poured into jars sterilised with boiling water. They placed a small wax disc over the cooling jam and cut out a pot cover from carefully saved scraps of brown paper, then tied with brown string.

Everything's breaking and he's also losing things. He writes this troubled letter:

M: *I cling to the things I have from you, from our time before we arrived here. Thank God all that's behind me, I ran around like a lunatic meshuggena,* (Yiddish word for a madman) *now I feel a bit better. Dumpling, it's time I came home, I'm all over the place, forget everything and lost first the pipe, then the ring and now the Parker pen. I work here like mad to keep myself occupied. Otherwise it wouldn't work. Then I would really go mad. I have three times as much to do as in Huyton. I'm unfortunately worked in here the officers know that and ask me everything. This does not hasten my release.*

And baby? It will be a boy after all! So Dumpling write to me soon and many good wishes to all, kisses for you

T: *My boy, it's dreadful this business about losing everything. We made a mistake that you didn't give me the things to take home. A simple dipping pen would have been sufficient.*

The main thing is that you come home safely, things are always replaceable. As long as you have my picture up and don't forget me, I'm writing often, I know what it's like waiting for letters. I ordered our pram. It'll all work out don't worry, I'll make sure of it.

He is also sending his washing home; implying that it's her duty as a good wife to do his laundry and darning.

M: *I have sent washing again. I could also let the laundry do it here. But first, it's not cheap, secondly you look after it better and I like wearing it if I know that you sewed the buttons on and no-one else. House work is house work. Meanwhile I got the parcel with the suit and shoes, but the braces are still not there.*

Thea's sardonic reply shows she understands that he needs reassurance that he is held in mind. At the same time she lets him know that domestic chores are not her favourite things,

T: *Send your washing frequently, My God, I love doing it!! Early this morning I sewed your buttons on…see I didn't forget.*

She describes detail about baby to involve him:

T: *Yesterday the Dr heard the tiny heartbeat; its little back is lying to the left instead of to the right. My blood pressure is a bit raised that's quite normal and the child is the right size. Now I have to take vitamin tablets, a combination pill of A,B,C and D, it's so that the baby grows strong and is protected against infections. Everything else needs to stop - calcium.*

This makes him long for a visit.

M: *You could visit whilst the weather is calm easily get here; but you never know so I guess I must wait until my release to see you. In that case send me my braces. But probably you won't want to come, or what??*

He refers to the weather again:

M: *Meanwhile I went to sleep and sit again in the office. Today the weather is stormy and the sea has high waves, which crash against the promenade, right under my window. Good that it's not Jerry*

Claude commented: Manfred was a man with not completely the foot on the earth - always a little bit higher. But to stay alive these Jews have to go on the earth; not a normal way feet on the earth. In an unsafe place, basic.

He is longing to see someone from home.

M: *You wrote about a visit from Harry on the horizon, but I guess nothing came of it. Perhaps it's better he stays in Leeds so at least there is a man there.*

Later he writes:

M: *Henry must decide on the special leave, whether we get permission; there's little point. I'm not bothered. I don't want leave I want my release.*

M: *Today is what one calls a glorious day; bright sunshine, blue sea and warm air - like in spring.*

M: *Yesterday we went for a walk, two hours in bright sunshine. It is actually as lovely as a picture postcard here. One could live here.... greetings to all*

M: *The weather is fine today and I shall probably go for a walk this afternoon with one of the officers.*

Today we are being taken to the cinema in town. It costs sixpence. We walk there in pairs a long crocodile, like children!

He makes fleeting references to camp life. He emphasises throughout the correspondence how hard he works to show he is conscientious and maybe showing the censor his commitment to serving the British army, indeed his commitment to becoming British.

In his more optimistic moods he is able to reflect more on the baby. Thea is concerned about choosing a name and that they belong to a Jewish community. She knows that if the baby is a boy he needs a circumcision and didn't realise the doctor would take charge.

T: *By the way thing about his names, I don't actually know your taste. We have often talked about it. I would like the first name to be something English and young, nothing heavy or old-fashioned. And the second name, perhaps Ernest because he will be English. Then girls' names, let me know your ideas. I must make contact with the Jewish community. We are not members at the moment and we should join before the baby arrives shouldn't we? Because of the brith* (circumcision) *Let me know whether you feel it's necessary to join or not.*

Claude: *Carry's mother organised, she does what has to be done. In every situation.*

M: *Did you get my washing? I'm a bit short of hankies and I've got a cold. When the men have a cold, the women have children.*

Dumpling, don't wind yourself up about the brith. (circumcision). Dr Rummelsburg will watch out and accompany the moel from shul. (Synagogue)He has done thousands of babies and nothing went wrong. If the Dr and Rabbi are together that's fine. In Berlin many doctors in the community were present like this. It's fine if Chazen, Stern or Apfel are there, or perhaps Frankel who knows us. That's it, love and kisses. Of course we should join a Jewish community, ring them up.

He has to ask for pocket money, like a schoolboy, a lack of dignity for a proud German who sees his role as a provider.

M: *By the way, if you can ----- a pound note, I would be very much obliged* (in English)

T: *Enclosed you will find the postal order, not ten shillings but a pound. Please confirm it at once.*

I've just spoken quite sharply to Henry (the solicitor) about my naturalisation and will write again for the hundredth time. Aunty Beattie got news today that she should send in her passport; it must soon be my turn.

At their marriage in Berlin, Thea was required to relinquish her British passport and adopt his German nationality. She was issued with a German passport embossed with a swastika. She had now applied for naturalisation to reclaim her British nationality.

M: *I am so angry I could explode; you won't get yours as long as I'm interned. Now sort it that I come home soon because it's nearly holidays*

M: *The weather is slowly turning to autumn. Today for example, it rains, though the sea is quite calm, but the sun is missing. It's not cold here, the opposite, palm trees even grow wild, it's like being in Italy. So for a holiday it's perfect.*

He misses his roommate Koenig, and he is very sad when his brother Kurt's release comes through and he leaves.

M: *So, Kurt travelled off early today and I am alone again in the office looking out to sea; the waves are high and the winds blowing. Quite romantic At least I am with you and the baby in my thoughts. But what use is that? In any case, not get emotional. I haven't given up yet.*

The importance of his walks becomes clear. His letters demand more and more; he is beginning to believe that he is nobody, that everyone can manage without him.

So there is another demand for food.

M: *Provisions are sparser here than in Huyton so I need a lot. For example, I would be very grateful for TOMAR (Kosher margarine) it can also be non-kosher if necessary. Cheese, sausage, bread, coffee, milk, cereal, chocolate, sardines, mixed pickles salad cream, Piccalilli, above all an electric plug as mine is broken, my braces (why am I asking for these since two months) and above all a homemade cake. I don't mind if Friedchen bakes it or a plum pudding to warm me and also boiled eggs.*

T: *Go careful with the margarine, I had to use our rations for you, so we are without 'till the end of the month. Let me know what you think of the eggs, they weren't fresh, and they were the ones we preserved from our own chickens. Did they taste alright? Did you fry them?*

M: *I just got a letter with a parcel. It'll be washing. Of course I'm careful with the margarine. You can send schmaltz. That'll keep.*

M: *My mother sent me yesterday a cold lambs tongue. That was a feast and it arrived safely.*

Thea takes the hint, cooks him a tongue and gives him reassurance.

T: *I've just put a tongue in the oven for my boy, I'll press it later and tomorrow it goes in the post. Let me know that it arrived and how it tasted. Tomorrow I'll also send washing,*

M: *The tongue was a brain wave. It was fabulous. The whole hotel talks about it.*

His home-cooked parcel demonstrates to his fellow internees that he is loved, that he has a home.

M: *Many thanks. Mornings, at breakfast I started to eat it, then during the day I nibble a bit here and there. It tastes so good.*

Thea makes a decision: to let their house.

T: *I let our house, furnished. I got so many offers, as there are hardly rooms available in Leeds, we have so many evacuees here. The empty house is damp and cold, now it will be clean and warmed through. My price was £3 per week but knocked off ten shillings as they have their own washing machine. They know that I want to be back there as soon as you come home. Weeks' notice and just think about it, I can save £2-10s-0p every week. Even if it's only three or four weeks, it would be ten pounds for us. At the moment I don't use any money. I didn't like having to make the decision without your opinion but I couldn't wait for your answer and you trust me, no? Also, a lot of soldiers are billeted in our area and if the house is empty it could be requisitioned, then we would not get it back when we want.*

I've been really busy, today we started cleaning it and I'm repairing the blackouts; which I was going to do for us anyway. They move in next Monday

When's your washing coming?

His only comment:

M: *My records, what about my records?*

He had left Berlin with just his collection of 78 records and a radio.

T: *My dearest boy the radio is here and the records all packed up with all our things in the Moth trunk in the box room, I can tell you we three women were so tired after working really hard the last four days . We were in bed by ten-thirty. Everything is clean, and perfect blackout everywhere; nicely ready for both of us. I'm really pleased I made the decision; I left every day crockery and household stuff.*

M: *My darling, it's 10am and I am sitting in my room and just about to rush off to work. It's really bad weather today, so unusual... It's a beautiful view outside the barbed wire and directly on the sea. This morning a pale watery yellow sun rose in the sky. From my window to the water is about 100 yards. Today the sea rocks violently and looks so high that ships aren't sailing, which means that there will be no post tomorrow, as it's the same boat that comes back to the island at night.*

The sequence of their letters is like the rolling waves, becoming increasingly disturbed as the nights draw in. Palm trees are blown sideways by biting wind on the promenade and the sunshine disappears. They are keeping warm by the little gas fire in the office, Douglas, and in front of the coal fire, Leeds. There are increased descriptions of food heated on the little electric plate. Mid-winter, a period of mourning and waiting, a winter of sirens and a baby kicking, she knitting, he watching his friends released one by one.

T: *We have terrible weather; I couldn't sleep at night because of the storm. Gretchen neither because of toothache, it's all nerves with her, she's still in pieces. I'm knitting again for the baby, a baby sleeping sack, then I have enough of small things. This is the last piece I'm knitting, it's time it comes out! He's so big and strong to carry around, I puff and huff like an old market woman, and waltz my body from side to side, it wants to come soon itself, I feel at night how it moves around, But it's still how wonderful nature works how the development of 9 months passes before you Now he soon won't belong to me alone, when he gets here you'll have your share, Pappi! Henry thinks it'll be a girl I've told everyone it's all the same to us. As long as it's healthy.*

Their correspondence is like a musical score, the base line a different tone to the melody line, often quite separate.

M: *Many thanks for the packet with rollmops. Is the Home Office aware that you are near giving birth? Don't be annoyed Dumpling, that I keep on, but if I'm not there for the birth, I don't know what I'll do. I MUST be there.*

In half an hour we are going to the cinema and I'll be pleased to have my mind taken off things. What date does the doctor think the baby will come? I'm so confused, is it December or January? I stick to John David and the third name, of course Ernest. Do you agree?

Dumpling, make sure you get rid of the cold; otherwise the baby will come into the world with a snotty nose.

T: *This morning I washed your beloved trousers and shirts! Now it's already five o'clock and I must get the letter into today's post. Then I'll stay in front of the fire. Your advice about walking is easier said than done, but I do it as much as I can...I was so pleased, boy, that your letter from the 6th sounded much more optimistic*

Between now and 3rd Jan the baby could come any time. If things would work out your release and the birth would be this side of the New Year. I have just heard about two boys who have returned. Everyone says the same, you have to convince them yourself that you still have pain from the operation. Sometimes I'm frightened when I think how I must manage without you, then I get more courage. Actually, I won't get soft, don't worry.

PS: listen you; I've saved guess how much - £23. Good eh? That'll be a nice little fund for us later.

M: *Believe me, Darling, I am not desperate and I don't lose my nerves.*

She replies:

T: *Today the first snow fell, everything is white and slippery. I daren't go past the front door alone; this is not the moment to fall; but Gretchen will go for a walk with me later on... Recently I dreamt that you came, I flung my arms round you but you didn't recognise me. It was dreadful; I'm fed up of all our acquaintances, including Webers. I like being with my Mum best or alone at home.*

We have all knitted so many baby things, My love I am so fed up, I am so homesick for you, if all our current efforts don't work Harry will visit you and discuss it further I need to put more coal on the fire.

Manfred notices that Thea's mood is sinking.

M: *Your letter sounded a bit depressed, not in the brightest mood. Soon it's your birthday. I am quite excited; my birthday letter will arrive punctually. Let's hope that we'll be able to celebrate in better circumstances next year. Also we already have wonderful memories; already I feel better when I think of them. Not long.... the idea of sending Morrison a telegram; perhaps a miracle might happen. Now, don't get soft. There's no point. Simply write to the Home Office over and over again. Don't let up. Write quite naturally and neutral and honestly. Perhaps we get lucky.*

Claude and I are transcribing and translating and discussing these bleaker letters and realise that Manfred was omitting his most significant personal experiences. Music was the main part of my father - why wasn't it on the page?

> *Claude later remarks: Carry's father doesn't write a word about music. He told her he went to concerts, yet he kept music completely separate; the meaning of this omission is perhaps the*

music was the spiritual part of her father. He didn't want to show it.

He was obliged to put his foot on the earth. In the mother's letters you can feel that. She says "you don't understand...You think it's so easy....to send margarine. We are sacrificing to send you...
She has to send him to reality.

Carry wanted to invent a letter describing the music. I said she can't do that, she has to write the truth of what is in the letters. Another truth (of the internment) is the music; she can't mix them, as her father didn't mix them in the letters.

At this point I wanted to step into this correspondence and make my young mother, whose spiritual side was embodied in her unborn baby, understand what was happening to my Dad. Claude persuaded me that my father needed to keep his spiritual side secret at that time and it was not my place to tamper with the truth.

Claude asked me to describe my grandmother's house, Southfield Drive, Moortown, Leeds 17. She lived there until her death, in 1960, when we were teenagers. Long after peace had broken out in Europe I would be pulled over our granny's fence by my impatient brother and run across the fields. I would stop in wooded areas, examine my grazed knees and be amazed at the cloud of bluebells in the long grass; Johnny would be shouting for me to follow, hurry, skim stones in the stream and back over the fence before anyone had noticed we weren't still playing marbles in the garden. We had been bathed in her tub and carried downstairs wrapped in a towel to be dried in front of the fire, then both of us tucked up in either end of her sofa to sleep.

Claude sits looking at the sloping handwriting on the envelope; the Sefton Hotel. We eventually visit.

Claude: The father gave a lot of description of activity of the camp - it would be interesting to see where it happened and the address of the Sefton Hotel, I read this address on every envelope - I would like to see this town, this street, this place.

113

*In one way I can understand - he was interned
and wanted to be free. When I saw Douglas I
thought this is not so hard to be interned here, I
imagined it would be harder.*

*The landscape, a sea view, you have an opening
to the sky, the sea, the world. I imagined him in
a cell with no view. When I heard about all the
activity and creativity on the island I thought
these were not such hard conditions.*

In the Sefton hotel in my attic room with a view,
which could have been his, I looked out on the horizon and
watched the ferryboats going backwards and forwards. But
he couldn't go.

They had enough food. At some level it was alright.
But they also didn't know what was going to happen. Would
England be invaded by the Nazis?

We are there, we have stayed in the Sefton Hotel, in the
same attic room, looking out to the sea.

Claude and Claudine paint pictures on the promenade,
they paint the sea, the horizon on a bright crisp autumn day.
Claude turns to me:

"You know the date?"

I shake my head.

"Today Manfred arrived here on the Isle of Man, it's the
day after Eugene's funeral."

Claude has drawn the promenade, the hotel without
barbed wire and gives the picture to me.

It's the 19th October.

"You can make new roots," he said to me, "but it's the
first roots that are the deepest."

Thea writes:

T: *Yesterday little Joan said to her mother "Aunty Theo got
so fat, she's got such a big tummy" But it was nice; the baby will
soon be there won't it. What do you think of that comment? I
think it's really sweet.*

M: *Tomorrow is Sunday again and I will spend a couple of
hours going for a walk I get extra privileges and don't have to go
in line with everyone.*

M: *The weather is now quite wintry and stormy, but in the office it's nice and warm. Send Thomas a Christmas card, but you noodle head will forget! And Riley. This sort of thing is important.*

She writes:

T: *Imagine beloved, the child is ready to come, he has everything and is waiting to come to the outside. It's an unbelievably wonderful thought, even if he has your thick head!*

Sometimes I think we have to be separated otherwise the good things would be overwhelming. We will be so happy when we can live together. God willing it will be healthy, write soon, when I don't hear you seem further away. Tummy bigger little one brings us luck I'm sure.

He writes:

M: *Yesterday your parcel with the chicken came. Yes, that was a joy! It was lucky that it was so cold and it kept wonderfully. I hung it out of the window at night and will prepare it tonight. Coincidentally it's Shabbos so that's good. I invited Kohut to eat it with me. I think I'll "schmoren", fry it. I'll tell you exactly what I did tomorrow. Will you eat Turkey for Christmas? Do I get a piece too?*

> Claude: *He couldn't write completely about what he wanted. Would he worry her? Did he have to say things were OK?*

Thea's birthday - 20ᵗʰ December.

T: *Fingers crossed, perhaps I'll get a surprise telegram from you. I keep hoping you'll know something about release before me. My Darling, first post brought your letter and the parcel arrived yesterday. I had a little cry, how silly I am! But next year we will be three. The little donkey from Daddy, is too sweet, it's really the first toy for our baby, to give it yourself. I was so pleased. And the shawl is really warm and pretty, so nicely woven. Charley is taking it to wash and dampen as he knows about weaving. I won't wear it till you're back, because I'm still wearing mourning I didn't expect anything except a letter, and even the red flowers were there, six beautiful dark red carnations from my lover!*

M: *When you get this your birthday will be over. Hope the cake tasted good. I assume that you'll send me a piece. And did you like the shawl? You must dampen it so that it gets soft. And the donkey is the first toy for the baby. Waxed cloth is very practical as you can spit on it and it simply washes off. And I hoped the flowers would be red roses? Next year, I'll do everything myself.*

She describes her birthday.

T: *My boy thank goodness my birthday's over; an event although I didn't want anyone to come. Lunchtime Lotte and Webers and Schlesinger and George and Beatty came and stayed for supper. At 8 o'clock the air raid sounded. Harry couldn't come because he had to go to his fire watch station on duty and seven of us sat in the shelter with our plates on our knees and one candle. I wore your shawl over my coat.*

At 11 the all clear sounded, apart from A Agnes there was nothing else here, thank God. Soon after my little brother arrived and bought me a box of asparagus and a bottle of Courvoisier. I'll wait till you're here for that. We got to bed around two. So beloved I kept hoping for a miracle to the last, moment. It shouldn't be this bad for the two of us. I'm thankful that you're doing OK and that you're not in danger. It's only the separation that's so difficult I keep telling myself it's not so bad. Eventually a reply will come and we must have patience. Harry wrote how difficult things are, no more Daddy, Gretchen not well, me not far from the birth and Harry responsible for everything. We just have to wait. Now do you want to know what presents I got?

From Harry a black bag, from Lotte a home-knitted bed jacket, because it'll be cold there; from Gretchen another bed jacket, one for day one for night at the hospital, and slippers and wool to knit a jumper for myself and a wonderful enormous nightshirt, wait till you see it! And a wooden stand with two jars for jam and marmalade, Aunty Beattie gave me a teckramen which she made herself, inlaid with wood. Uncle George patterned hankies and the same from Sybil, Friedchen gave me a rubber apron for bathing the baby and a little jacket and two pairs of shoes she knitted for the baby, so sweet, Lotte Kremer a baby hair brush, Beherendts a baby spoon, Webers a wallet where I'll put all the pounds I'm saving; you can see baby got as much as me! I'm enclosing a pound postal order, Christmas present from Gretchen so loved one be good and love me for the next fifty years lots of kisses Lump

He receives her birthday cake and Hanukah parcel

M: *The chocolate cake is quite wonderful. Did Frieda bake it? Many thanks for the £2 from Gretchen and you. I don't know who I should thank first. I'm pleased that your birthday went well, even though I wasn't there. And you got enough useful presents. I already wrote to you that there will be a H.O. question session here next Wednesday. I advise you to emphasise hardship and at present the H.O. favours hardship cases.*

T: *My beloved Pappi, now Christmas is past and I didn't write to you over the two holidays. Yesterday your sweet Hanukah card arrived, it was delightful,*

Yesterday I got a letter from the Home Office, my request for you to undergo a physical examination is under consideration and they have asked for a report from the camp. Perhaps you could hurry things up; I don't see why it should take months. It should just work. Stress the hernia story and everything else that's not right. Harry wrote about the hardship case, but you know the HO won't be persuaded if one whines and complains too much. They do nothing and then there's never a release telegram.

We're both tough and don't let things get us down. And when our child arrives everything will go right. I am fantastic, I feel better now than I did over the last nine months. Everyone says I look better than I did the whole time.

He has heard about air raids in Manchester, is now worried about his parents.

M: *Have you heard from Manchester? It must look dreadful there. Hopefully, everything is OK .*

T: *Just Yesterday I spoke on the phone with Kurt and immediately sent you a telegram saying that everything is OK in Manchester. I thought you might be worried when you hear about the air-raids. He promised to write a card every two days, so I'm in constant contact.*

She is desperately trying to get his release.

T: *My boy, please, please do everything you can for the reports from the H.O. This is our big chance... We must have* patience, whilst it's being processed and Henry has asked again in a letter. But your examination is as important.

He is increasingly despairing.

M: *I must surely be home for Christmas. He shouldn't wait till he hears but send a telegram asking why the silence. The hardship stuff is my last hope. I don't build much on the medical, particularly if it takes so long.*

She struggles to keep going

T: *Your low spirits don't help me at all. I have to hold my head high and get on with it. No one who is released is surprised at the way you write. You are still in limbo. An answer must come soon from the H.O., this way or that. There are two hopes. Let me have a healthy baby first, then Harry will visit you if we haven't heard by then. I have not forgotten about it, but at the moment I can't handle it, do you understand? Keep your head high, my loved one, I also am finding it all hard..*

He just manages to think about her and now will even entertain the idea of special leave for the birth rather than release.

M: *So how are you otherwise? When are you going to the nursing home? I'm also constantly dreaming now about it - but everything goes well in the dream. Only when I awake I'm fed up and waiting for a miracle. There's not a lot we can do. In a few days I'll have the medical. Special leave is usually granted in special circumstances. But it's not like Huyton, the HO isn't here and must notify Henry, and then he needs an answer. You can have three children by the time all this is done. So, write me soon that I'm in the picture, you must still have washing, and I'm running out of hankies.*

She turns her attention back to the baby

T: *Visited our doctor again. He was as satisfied with me. Everything's as it should be; another heart examination and urine test. Another week and it'll be ready my love, and so sure that the future is going to bring us everything good. When the little one arrives everything will work out for us. This conviction is helping me overcome our dreadful separation. And you should feel the same yes?*

He is desperate now and considers enlisting for the army.

M: *I must say, I can't see a way out anymore. My release will depend on joining the Pioneer Corps. I think there's a chance* to join the people who want to stay in England. I'll give it some thought, I can't stand staying here much longer. Many greetings to all and lots of kisses for you.

She tries to cheer him up.

T: *The reality is that you are always with me and me with you. We have with God's help our future before us. And the three of us, with our child is a wonderful thought. Who knows, when you get these few lines you'll already have news. But no, the letter is in the post less than the week.*

The hospital is in Harrogate Road, just before you come to Chapeltown Road, You know where the fire station is and the school is on the right if you're coming from us. It's between them, a bit set back. Very pretty, in a garden. My room is big, in comparison, I mean, not modern, but nice, As soon as the pains start I'll drive there with my little case... and the doctor says it takes longer with the first one. You can reckon the whole day, tomorrow I'll send you your washing, and I did all the ironing myself this time. I'll send you some fried potatoes and a little piece of goose, so you can also taste it. Very good.

He only writes about food.

M: *Perhaps a miracle might happen. What kind of room will you have in the nursing home? Did you speak with Rummelsbourg...what will one eat after the brith? We need to think of everything. God will help. Yesterday I got a piece of goose and a glass of chocolate pudding. That of course made a wonderful supper! If boxes are heavy, don't bother to send them. We get enough food here. What I need is just cold stuff for supper, like sausage and cold meat, perhaps a bit of ham, for example the liver sausage was a good idea. And I like to heat up some soup in the evening.*

T: *I'm, touch wood, fine. I feel better than I did the last six months. The doctor reckons you can't be too accurate with the first one. It's so weird, everything is prepared and ready and I have the feeling tomorrow I might not be here anymore.*

M: *Tonight is Christmas Eve and first night of Hanukah. In an hour we will have coffee and cakes in the hotel and afterwards we will light the candles. And tomorrow I'm pleased that there won't be much to do in the office because of the holidays. No letter or parcel came from you today, pity, but its sure to be because the post is delayed. And what do we hear from the Home Office? Nothing of course. I can't imagine that you should have a baby and I can't be with you. In any case I'm always with you in my thoughts and pray that everything will go well. When will this situation change? It'll be good again somehow.*

She writes:

T: *Yesterday your letter of 24th arrived; I was pleased to see everything had arrived. You didn't mention the plum pudding and cream? Delicacies today*

A group of internees send a telegram to the Home secretary:

```
            Telegram
Herbert Morrison,
Home secretary
Whitehall


Sir, undersigned internees whose reports
fully prove their sincerity appeal to your
generosity and kind heart stop Our wives
are expecting first babies near Christmas
stop. We implore you to fulfil our most
ardent Christmas wish to be with our wives
at their most critical hour stop
Manfred Gornitzky stop Hubert Schwarz stop
Paul Geiger stop Herbert Cohn stop Arnold
Gottlieb stop Seftoncamp Douglasman
```

M: *If nothing happens by the New Year, I'll go to the AMPP. What do you all think? In any case I have no desire to sit here for ever.*

T: *Happy New Year my loved one, please God that the New Year brings us more luck and joy than the last one. Otherwise I wish us both so much that words can't express it. Don't you agree? And you my boy, did you go to sleep early last night? That's the most sensible so as not to be over whelmed by the feelings.*

M: *It's again post time. Every morning I'm asked if you are in labour. And I have no idea. I sit here, know nothing and could have become a father overnight. Ah, pudding, it's weird. Are the home office aware that you are near giving birth? Don't be annoyed pudding that I keep on but if I'm not there for the birth.... I MUST be there.*

Manfred received a telegram giving him news of his son's birth on 9th January 1941.

Manfred received his release telegram on 10th January 1941.

Two weeks later he received a letter from the Commanding Officer who was responsible for his release and apologising for the delay. Apparently, through a clerical error, he was classified as higher risk than other Jewish internees.

Claudine watched Claude entering, or as she said, intruding into their lives. I sometimes sat at their kitchen table discussing a phrase or two. When I arrived one evening, "Here you are ....a special Isle of Man need," she said, putting a plate of rollmops on the table!

"Part of your mittel Europa history is also part of me." Shoots of friendship across time.

Manfred walked along the Douglas promenade, his precious hot plate safely under his arm to the ferry waiting to take him across the Irish Sea to Liverpool.

He'd walk to Lime Street station and then, at last, he would be on the train home to Leeds. Turning his collar up against the wind whipping his face, he decided he would describe the Isle of Man as fun, a Holiday Camp, thank you British government for keeping me safe.

Only many years after his death, would I unravel his stories. What it meant to be stripped of national identity and freedom would only be revealed in these letters tied together with brown string.

She puts her finger to her lips, the caramel dog must remain silent; both stand very still listening to the conversation, the language is bird.

She makes a paper bird, decorated with her dreams and wishes painted on the side. It has an open beak to be filled with air as she runs, her kite on a long string flying behind her.

The kite is high in the blue sky. A gust of wind, it blows stronger. Zero's wishes flutter, she releases the string, they are carried far away...

The leaves vibrate with birdsong, excited blue tits chatter as they steal overripe cherries from branches at the top of the tree, red juice dribbling down tiny feathered chests.

PART THREE

I come into the story

In the mine of my heart a spark hides –
not large, but wholly my own.
Neither hired, nor borrowed, nor stolen –
my very own.
Chaim Bialik

Chapter 7

Salford. Manfred is sitting in Mama's kitchen. It is the spring equinox and the light is leaving a sky streaked with pink and lilac as if painted with a toddler's chubby fingers. He watches his mother make tea. She pours the black liquid into two glasses and adds a spoonful of strawberry jam.

His parents are contemplating another emigration, to join their daughter in South Africa. Mama's sight is weakening. The smell of chicken soup bubbling on the stove reminds him of life in Berlin. His mother stirs the soup. He asks if she put a beef bone in the broth to strengthen the flavour. She nods smiling, delighted that he remembers her old trick.

"I can't always get one now," she says. "I've found a kosher butcher here in the neighbourhood, but with rationing it's hard to get a good bone, with any meat remaining. Besides, if Papa isn't with me they don't understand what I'm saying." Mama has found learning English very difficult.

Manfred watches his mother moulding a matzo ball between her hands, a light mix of schmaltz and fine matzo meal. She runs cold water over the round shape and places it on the scrubbed wooden board that also makes him think of the Berlin kitchen.

She looks up. "I learned this recipe from my mother-in-law; I always hoped one of my daughters-in-law would be interested so I could pass it on to the next generation."

Thea's lack of interest in a Jewish way of life had always disappointed his mother. Indeed, neither my Mum nor my Aunty Helga had delivered the traditional Jewish home life she had wished for her two sons. She was unaware that even in Berlin Manfred had been pulling away from her Orthodox way of life. At that time he was influenced by the period of Enlightenment and the belief that German and Jewish identities could co-exist harmoniously. Those days had long gone up in the smoke rising from crematorium chimneys across Europe. Manfred would eventually join the Reform synagogue in Leeds. His priority was for his children to take their place in secular society and contribute to peace and tolerance in post-war Leeds.

"Maybe if we have a girl this time...."

"You'd like a girl?" she asks.

He nods. "The boy, you know I feel the odd one out. Maybe it's because I wasn't there when he was growing. I was far away, and I never really got a chance, he never knew my voice before he came into the world, sometimes I still feel he doesn't know me."

"It'll be different you'll see. This new child will even things out, there'll be four of you."

She peers out of the window in her horn-rimmed spectacles. The grey Salford drizzle has made the pavements shiny, darkness is falling.

"Manfred, go to Leeds, that's where your home is now, go, she needs you there. You don't want to miss this birth, the new child needs to see you as soon as it arrives. You need to see each other! *Manfred, das kind wird balt da sein* the child is coming, go home to greet it." At that moment the phone rings. My mother's contractions have started.

"I'm on my way." He kisses his mother and leaps down the steps two at a time, pulling on his coat. "Wish us luck," he calls over his shoulder and runs for his train.

I am born.

The women are sitting knitting in the front room. Occasionally they glance up at the daffodils outside the bay window. My mother's waters break, she puts her knitting down and phones the midwife, then my father, before running a warm bath.

My great aunt Frieda picks up the knitting, a shawl, the first fabric my skin will touch, and continues at high speed.

That spring most babies were born in hospital as there was an epidemic of gastro-enteritis. Mothers looked on helplessly as their babies slowly died of dehydration. My mother persuaded her doctor to allow a home birth.

My father sits on the top step in front of the closed door, waiting. My mother pushes me into the world. I arrive with ear piercing cries. I am wrapped in the shawl.

The door opens and my father reaches out his arms. He sits on the step, tears rolling down his cheeks, as he holds me in his arms. He has an English daughter. I was the baby born to peace, six weeks before Victory in Europe, VE day.

Granny carried my sleeping brother to our parents' bed to make room for my arrival during the night. At two o'clock in the morning, she changed my first nappy. Later she made my brother's breakfast and put me in his arms for a few moments before he set off for nursery. He was on his tricycle, four-year-old legs pedalling furiously, our great aunt Frieda running behind shouting in German, trying to fasten her hat pin which had come loose, handbag swinging, begging him to slow down. *"Johnnyschen, langsamm, langsamm, du gehst zu schnell, ach du lieber Gott."*

He was already forging the path I would soon be following, always trying to keep up.

As soon as I was big enough he would let me sit on the saddle of his bike, whilst he pedalled standing up. We climbed the hill. At the top he'd shout over his shoulder, "Hold on tight." My arms would tighten round his waist, my face pressed into his jumper and we were off, top speed down the hill. Later he taught me to ride my own bike and led me safely through the streets to our Gran. We had to cross the tramlines in the middle of the road.

"Careful," he called. "Don't let the wheels catch in the grooves."

Too late, I'd fallen, trapped underneath my bike, weeping. He glanced down the road; the tram was shuddering round the corner slowly advancing on us.

"Lift your bike," he said gently.

I wiped my nose on my cardigan sleeve and lifted my bike.

"Now stand up."

I was shaking.

"Look right, left, right and come across if it's clear."

I obeyed his instructions and walked towards him, a hug and a gob-stopper as a reward for being sensible and staying calm. From then on I'd always trust his judgement.

"Matters," he would say. "We have matters to discuss."

My heart sank. I was a puppy with a perpetually guilty conscience. He would list my misdemeanours:

Pinching a piece of chocolate (doled out weekly because there was still rationing);

Holding back a threepenny bit from my dinner money change;

Sticking my tongue out behind my Mum's back;

Pretending I was constipated and sitting on the toilet with a book to avoid the washing up.

These offences required handing over some of my pocket money otherwise he'd tell and I'd have 'had it'.

Discussing "matters" sometimes felt important and exciting. We'd pool our information on the "war", what had happened "before", what was the number on Uncle George's arm? Why did Aunty Lotte never mention her mum and dad?

If I didn't dream at night I would daydream during the day. I sometimes dreamt of forests, the setting of the fairy stories by the Brothers Grimm. The pines growing close together with white barks chewed away by hungry deer in the midst of icy winters, driven down from the safety of high ground by hunger. The trees grow close together and shafts of sunlight slant across the clusters of trees. A sandy floor strewn with needles; cool and dark, dry twigs snap underfoot. Silence.

It's where the wild things are, watching, as we walk through, startled, as I pull my sweater over my head and feel the rabbit's tail in my pocket. We are sucked towards darkness. What does the forest mean to us both? Hiding? Shooting?

The secrets and silences around us were at the heart of what mattered to us. Our 'matters' also contained our own secrets and silences. We hatched elaborate plans to keep Johnny's detentions secret from our father. Trouble at school, his undone homework, caught for smoking, insolence. He was the captain, conspiring against authority, I was his loyal lieutenant.

My 'matters' concerned losing my swimming costume, a sock, dinner money and the sixpence we carried to school every Monday for the teacher to put in the Yorkshire Penny Bank. My losing stuff helped his excuses for being late at school. He was always late; he was searching for his sister's boot.

"Boot Gorney?"

"Yes sir, a boot."

"How could she lose one boot?"

"I dunno sir, she'd lose her head if it weren't stuck on, sir. That's what our Mam says."

I am a little sister playing. He measures me under a tree, showing me how much space I take up in the world. I am the one who gets away with it, allowed to be myself, a sprite in a blue dress with smocking and a peter pan collar. Johnny takes carefully measured steps; he looks over his shoulder to make sure I'm following. I hop, skip, jump behind. Johnny was the bridge between the world of our family and everything else. He reached out his hand to help me gingerly step through our front door to England.

My brother John Ernest was the firstborn. Still in the war, he was the baby born to fulfil a refugee family's dreams. He heard the air-raid sirens. He heard the chatter of women, the clatter of knitting needles, the crackle of wrapping brown paper parcels and the sound of pots washed in the sink. He was the one who offered to wash up, I resisted. He held my mother's hand when I, ten days old, was whisked to hospital in an ambulance wrapped in a red blanket. He was a toddler watching. I became a toddler watching him.

I watch old footage of the coronation, sixty years ago, and remember us in our living room, lunch on our knees. Our family saved up sixpences for our first television in time for the coronation. I was given a glass coronation beer mug and a coin engraved with an image of the new queen.

I wasn't even aware that there were street parties taking place around Britain, I guess my parents didn't know what a street party was. They moved from apartment houses in Berlin to neat semis in Leeds, but stayed tightly within the family circle. They couldn't imagine themselves part of any community, English or Jewish.

Johnny refused to stand up for the national anthem, saying it was stupid in our front room and we weren't English anyway. I agreed, although no one noticed I was still sitting, or seemed interested in my opinion. I have never stood for the national anthem since.

My father hit Johnny, he hit back, my mum whisked me out of the room. I sat on the top step waiting. I missed the actual bit where the crown, with fur and jewels was placed on her head and everyone cheered "God Save the Queen". I just sat on the step, ate my crunchy bar and drew pictures of her dress instead.

My parents sold the family silver, carefully smuggled out of Germany, to pay for my brother to attend a Quaker boarding school. It was an attempt to join the English middle classes.

"The Quakers were good to us," my father used to say.

"Why do we need anyone to be good to us?" we discussed in Matters. My parents drove to York every Sunday to bring him home for the day. My Gran invited me to stay with her. I refused and sat alone in the back of the car waiting for him to jump in so we could resume our secret routines. He was silent, I kept prodding him, he moved further away. I whispered a rude German word; he pretended not to hear. I emptied my pocket of all its treasures, two boiled sweets, a threepenny bit, a pencil stub and a broken powder compact I had fished out of a dustbin. He sucked the sweets and pocketed the threepenny bit. I searched my brain for the naughtiest word I knew. With a deep breath and thudding heart I shouted "Fuck" as loudly as I could. Deathly silence. I glanced across. Johnny was smiling, so we were still friends.

He hated that school, he was the only Jewish boy, so he decided to hate being Jewish too. After two years he left and went to the local boys' grammar school near our house. Four years later I reached my goal, the girls' school next door.

Inside and outside

Members of the Jewish refugee community supported each other. They lived near each other, they took care of each other's children; they were very different from the English

Jews in Leeds who 'belonged', having arrived a hundred years previously. Our dentist was Viennese. His wife baked exquisite poppy seed and apple cake. When she knew we were having our teeth checked, she would leave some slices in the waiting room. My mother wrapped them in a hankie and took them home for tea.

Dr Schiller beamed at us, his waxed, walrus moustache quivered. His gold tooth gleamed as he settled us in his huge chair. His foot worked the pedal, the chair would tilt us until we were lying down quaking with terror as he raised his enormous, metal hypodermic needle, tapped its glass window before injecting its liquid into our gums. He barked scary German commands at us, while working on our teeth.

"Still halten!" (sit still}

"Spűlen!" (rinse out)

"Schpuken!" (spit) We didn't understand so he'd shriek over the drill, which sounded as though it was breaking up a slab of concrete "Shpit, shpit, mein Kind, no vurry, the blut vill stop soon."

Every week we had piano lessons with Frau Schiff. She lived in a large terrace house in Harehills. We opened the letterbox and found her key fastened to a piece of string. She lived right at the top. We raced each other up the stairs and gulped down the orange squash she gave us on arrival.

She would sail towards me like the battleship Potemkin, a huge bosom with a pince-nez resting on it and a large shelf-shaped bottom. She had a crooked mouth, maybe no teeth and her grey hair in a net. She taught us in German. She'd grip my arm and sit me down at the piano, whilst at the same time pressing a biscuit into Johnny's hand. I practised scales and then munched whilst listening to Johnny launch into a faltering Strauss Waltz. Soon he absconded, pocketing the money for lessons and swearing me to secrecy. I practised diligently between lessons, but never made much progress beyond *Twinkle, Twinkle Little Star.*

Cake Shops

I contributed a proportion of my silver sixpence pocket money to subsidise Johnny's and my visit to the cake shop on the parade near school. The man behind the counter filled a glass each with pop or Tizer. We returned the empty glass and he would swirl it around a bowl of warm water ready for the next customer.

There were magical English cakes. Eccles cakes cost a penny, sugary pastry cases stuffed with inky fruit jam. Genoa slabs had fat glace cherries embedded in the mix. Battenbergs were little squares of pink and gold sponge, topped with a coat of pink icing. Currant buns, long éclairs coated with thick chocolate or coffee icing cost tuppence, I would be allowed to lick them first before Johnny attacked the doughy mass inside. If we only had a penny between us the man would hand us a tin of broken biscuits and we were allowed to grab a handful. Sometimes we would share a friend's iced bun in school, with a spread of marge in the middle. On the street we'd pick the fruit out with our teeth or fingers and stuff the rest in our mouths pushing and shoving each other down the street.

My idea of exotic food was a sausage roll, flaky pale pastry with a small sausage lurking inside. My mother didn't even know they existed. I accompanied her to the local bring and buy sale or Beetle drive. Everyone sat in teams of four, given paper and dice. There was an entrance fee that went to help starving children in Africa. After the game, tea and cakes were served. I helped my Mum carry her cake tins and hand out cups of tea.

I was very interested in the other English cakes. Coffee walnut cake, made with Camp coffee, had a bitter taste that contrasted with the thick butter smeared on top, was a favourite. Fat chocolate truffles were coated in vermicelli, which I surreptitiously picked off whilst arranging them on plates.

1956

On a damp Tuesday afternoon in Leeds, freezing February, sometimes in thick yellow smog, the smell of burning yellowed leaves, we walked down the hill, clutching library books. This was our fortnightly visit to return our books before incurring a fine. My Mum went into the adult section. She pointed to the large clock with Roman numerals over the door.

"Ten minutes," she said, "when the big hand is on nine." I followed her finger carefully. "We can't stay longer today I haven't bought anything for tea yet."

I skipped into the children's section. I had been engrossed in a series on twins from different countries by Lucy Fitch Perkins I knelt by the bottom shelf leafing through the ones I hadn't yet read. I picked up the Japanese Twins, Taro and Take, opening it at the page when their new baby brother is born. Their father makes Take kneel down on the floor so that he can place the baby's foot on her neck. Then he makes her promise to obey the baby always, for he is a male and Take is 'only' a girl.

It's not fair, I thought, why do girls always come off worst?

My mum waited as the librarian stamped the book.

"Why aren't girls as good as boys?" I asked her as she took my hand, crossing the road to the butcher's.

"What do you mean?"

I told her about the book.

"Rubbish," she said, with her Berliner sharpness (quatsch), "that's a long way away, different countries have different customs, but it's different here. You could do the same as any boy, better even, just do well at school, you'll see..."

School? I'd stopped learning my times-tables by heart, our teacher only checked the boys. I chose not to mention this and wondered if girls became more important after the 11+ exam. What if I went to the girl's only school, near our house? Then girls would have to be important. I liked that idea. I found boys in our class a bit stupid, they were always fighting or shouting or looking for conkers. In class, when the answers came into my head and my hand shot up, the teacher often ignored me, choosing one of the boys.

A chilly snobbishness and a hint of anti-Semitism rustled in the undergrowth of the predictable world of Roundhay, the Leeds suburb where my parents improbably found themselves after their youth spent in Berlin. I already sensed that the grip of post-war respectability, toasting the queen, sitting with knees primly pressed together and wearing little white gloves was a way of women being repressed, controlled and subordinated. The hushed tones and neat blouses of my friends' mothers made me unsure of my own mother's assurance that I would be able to spread my wings. Without recognising it I was already preparing myself for the great elsewhere.

***

We were growing up in the fifties, in the context of post war stability, a boom, 'there'll always be an England'. Our parents were blocking out the horrors of World War Two and were desperate to prevent us from knowing about the death camps, the lives cut short by falling bombs, the bodies that remained buried. Our parents had been young adults in the war, fighting overseas, having babies in the blitz, food rationing. They lived in fear every night with the sound of sirens, sleeping on the platforms of the underground shoulder to shoulder with other traumatised neighbours. Stumbling out at daylight they feared their houses might no longer be standing. Now they hoped nothing would happen. They were relieved to sit in the suburbs and only think about a new twin tub washing machine and a quiet afternoon playing cricket. We were to become a generation simmering with an unspent energy underneath the boredom of predictable childhoods. We children of the fifties learnt to listen carefully and do well at school. We were the first to be treated by a new NHS. We were given NHS orange juice at nursery and free milk at school. If we were clever enough we would be entitled to a free further education, we stayed in school till we were sixteen.

We became the generation who chose not to hold a grownup's guiding hand to lead us from the silent, suburban, stifling fifties into the decade we would call our own. We were the generation bored with silence, predictability and the luxury of a new hostess trolley. We no longer wanted to hang our poplin non-iron shirts to drip-dry over the bath, we would loosen, indeed discard, our girdles, we would stride to our destiny in Doc Martins, not mince in kitten heels.

We had all been raised with descriptions of the war spirit, the make do and mend, the implied creativity that lay behind the untold stories of war, fear, bombs falling, prisoner of war camps and mass destruction. Our glimpses of the war were dark and grimy images, evil had risen out of the earth and was scrubbed and polished by the blooming affluence of the fifties. Our neat semi-detached houses seemed indestructible with their Formica tabletops and clean lino floors. Our parents had become fossilised with cabinet TVs.

We were a generation raised by traumatised parents, in a conspiracy of silence.

My father's monster, like a tiger, was always real, menacing, about to rip his life apart. He knew it had arrived when he stood at the window of his auntie's Berlin flat watching two little girls on a yellow bench. All through his life, this tiger hid in our coalhouse, under our stairs, creeping up on him, surprising him, with shouting, screaming, raging, smacking.

My father's terrible rages were tornadoes, sweeping through the house. The sudden eruptions rattled the bannister. We would all scatter. I hid under the roof of the piano keys, curled up as small as possible. I knew it would pass. I waited for him to crash his hands down on the keys, loud chords shuddering through the old black casing. He kept playing, I waited, a silent mouse. The thunderstorm was played out across the keys, slowly becoming quieter until I recognised the tune of the Brahms lullaby. He played it a few times and then bent down to pick me up and carry me off to bed. I never understood how he knew I was there. But my father lacked confidence when negotiating with authority. He stayed on the edge of society as Jews had for many generations, running their own businesses outside the mainstream. Often it was the only means they had of earning a living, all they were allowed to do. My father didn't want to embarrass me with his strong accent, so my mother went alone to school parents' evenings. "It made us seem more English," he said.

When we were on a train, going to Rhyl to visit a cousin, I sat looking out of the train window, dangling my legs and squinting in the light. "Mum," I asked. "Mummy, if you and I would have been on that train going to the camps and I would have been a baby, would you have thrown me out of the window? Would you have thrown me out so that a stranger could catch me?"

I studied her face closely. She didn't say anything, just looked out of the window at the Welsh countryside, the rolling hills, the sheep, her green eyes following the scenery.

My desire was a rabbit's tail. I drove my mother to distraction begging for a little white circle of fluff, like a netsuke to carry in my pocket so I could touch it at any moment.

"Please," I begged her. "Please, I NEED it."

I held the string shopping bag open for the brown paper packet of stewing steak whilst my Mum fished out 7/6d from her purse.

"Have you any beef bones?" she asked. He wrapped up a pile of red gnarled bones. "Thruppence please. Are they for the dog?"

"No, they make a good stock."

"You foreigners, it's like the war, always using the last bits."

That was the moment she asked for the rabbit tail, tucked in amongst the bones. She would wash it repeatedly until it was soft and white, ready to slip into my mitten when I walked to school. Neither of us would mention it again. I still have it.

Everything exciting had happened before I was born, my parents' life in Berlin, escaping, my father interned, even my brother's birth had sounded like an adventure in a hospital with air raid sirens going off, whereas I had been born at home and nothing special had happened. I'd have to wait for my adventures until I was old enough to leave. Foreignness like my auntie's laughter and intense conversations was desirable. Women's voices cascading with emotions erupted suddenly and burst explosively into the surface of life.

I was already aware that all this made us foreigners in Yorkshire, which seemed like cold air in front of your mouth on a winter's day. Emotion was firmly kept below the surface, maybe a word or two was spoken, at most a sentence, shoulders stiffened, certainly no wild arm movements.

My mother had had her own training for Yorkshire in her adolescence. She spoke quietly and she didn't like it when I shouted or screamed, but her voice did rise an octave or two when she slid into German, telling a joke, reading a book, talking and laughing with her Aunties. She saw herself as English, she embraced the Yorkshire in her background, took us for long walks on the moors, always a border collie cross running alongside.

"Foreigners Mum, are we foreign?" This was a new idea for me; maybe we could be exotic like the families in my twins' books.

"No," she said. "You're English, Daddy used to be foreign."

I stretched my hand over my heart. Was I English in there? I asked myself, through and through, maybe there was a bit of foreignness somewhere.

"Mum," I said swinging the string bag as we walked back up the hill. "I want to be an explorer."

"That's a good idea. What do you want to explore?"

"People," I answered. "I want to go to different countries and explore people."

I was thinking of the twins from different countries.

"You can explore people on your own street. Everyone's different."

That was boring, most people here looked the same dressed the same, spoke the same, except us.

"I want to be where everyone's different."

"As long as you can come home, as long as you know where home is." I knew where home was at that moment, watching her turn her key in the door and dropping to my knees to hug Toby dog who bounded towards us.

Of course I knew where home was.

I am balanced on my father's arm as he lights the Hanukah candles. He is singing. Behind him, stands my grandmother, behind her, great aunts and uncles. They all sing a Hebrew song, giving thanks for a light that long ago kept burning for eight days. Our room is flooded with candles.

Enthralled, I reach out and touch my father's face whilst he is singing, my fingers fluttering on his lips trying to catch his words. I twist round to watch my smiling, singing family giving thanks for eternal light. It is darkest mid-winter in Yorkshire.

Infant School

Johnny leads me over the bridge and across the field into England on my fifth birthday, still wearing my winter liberty bodice to keep warm. It's my first day at school. We stand in long rows. I am unable to spot my brother across the playground. Mr Chaplin, the head teacher walks along the rows checking names. He stops in front of me.

"You're new?" I nod my head. He smiles down at me and slips a penny into my hand, because I was so small. I wasn't a bit scared.

Sometime later Miss Madison with a moustache, asked me to repeat father's name, Manfred, in front of the class.

"That's a funny name," she said. "Is it foreign? Come and write it up on the board."

"Where did he come from?" she kept asking.

"Germany," I muttered, cheeks scarlet with shame. "But he's not really German. Well he is, and he isn't."

140

This was 1950 and the war was still fresh in everyone's mind. The Germans were baddies. We fought them in our playground games. Later we'd whistle the Dam Busters march and make up songs about Himmler who had no balls at all. We barked the German words we'd picked up in the films about the war. German was the language of the oppressors and yet it was the language of the nursery rhymes that had been sung to me when I'd sat on my father's knee. Germans were the enemy. Yet German was always waiting to welcome me indoors.

I knew they were my father's enemy; he was a German Jew, the Germans were the enemy of German Jews. I was certain about this, as certain as I was about lighting the candles on a Friday night. But I was five and it was too hard to explain. I just felt otherness. I was part of my father and yet totally different from him. I knew I absolutely was not German and yet I was part of a German family, who'd had to run away from Germans.

Infant School 1950

Carry aged 8

Rainbow knitting

The earth is enriched with the dust of the millions
of knitters who have held wool and needles since the
beginning of sheep. One likes to believe that there is
memory in the fingers; memory undeveloped, but
still alive.
Elizabeth Zimmermann
Elizabeth Zimmermann's Knitter's Almanac

Oberlin, an 18th century early years educationalist invented "the knitting stove". In Alsace, during the long cold winter, very young children warmed themselves around the stove while they practised knitting and were encouraged to tell each other stories. Like me, they flourished through the intimacy created by women calmly focusing on the repetition of stitches. Like me, whilst using their hands, they were opening their minds and spirit.

For centuries women incarcerated in mental hospitals furiously purled and knitted away the years. Knitting became a

142

subversive activity; heads bent over the busy needles appeared harmless. But wherever there was a knitting circle, the yarn connected people as well as stitches. The warp and weft form scaffolding to support a piece of fabric which appears as if by magic. Suddenly it is transformed into a three-dimensional garment. There is always hope for transformation.

Cafe Klatches with knitting were at the heart of my life as a child. The assortment of émigré aunties from the old days in Berlin, met regularly around our Formica kitchen table.

The aunties travelled across Leeds on the rattling maroon tram. They walked up the hill, puffing and panting in voluminous winter coats, hats, gloves, scarves, string shopping bags containing their knitting and handbags to hold their cigarettes, lighters and powder compacts. My mum filled the blue plastic electric coffee percolator with huge amounts of freshly ground coffee, the smell filled the house, welcoming the aunties as they came through the door. A home-baked cake was just out of the oven, still warm and crumbly when sliced.

These women were in their fifties and sixties, had lived their lives in Germany, working in shops, as book-keepers, as Montessori teachers. Some had never married, being the youngest, looking after an ageing parent, or they had loved and lost fiancés, husbands and even their adult children before their emigration. Their property was seized and belongings confiscated by the Nazis. They could leave with little more than the clothes on their backs. My aunties had smuggled their jewellery in their underwear, nailed into the soles of their shoes, sewn into the linings of their coats and of course they always had some knitting to keep their hands busy as they waited for safer times.

They were granted an entry visa if they had a guarantor already living here. The only work permit they received was as a home help. They felt they had no right to ever speak about what happened to them, because in their eyes nothing had happened to them, compared to the millions lost. They were the lucky ones, saved by a twist of fate.

This story of exile was like a piece of wobbly knitting with giant holes of dropped stitches, impossible to mend. They knitted two together but could never hide the gaps. The warp and weft was irrevocably damaged. Assuming the mantle of Englishness meant they loved the royal family. They discussed the king's abdication, Wallace Simpson's wardrobe. They debated Princess Margaret's violet eyes and later her doomed relationship with Peter Townsend. "Such a handsome man!" they exclaimed, cackling with laughter.

They made us write 'happy birthday' letters to the royal children. Sitting at the kitchen table, slowly ruling lines across small pieces of blue Basildon Bond paper for Princess Anne and Prince Charles. We wrote in neat round letters trying not to smudge the blue ink, careful not to press too hard on the fountain pen nib. A typewritten reply came through the post with a royal crest. I hated those two smug children, their coats with velvet collars. Nothing to do with me, I stuck my tongue out at their smiling faces in the papers. The tearaway heroines in books such as *Anne of Green Gables* or *Little Women* were the characters I wanted to emulate, independent heroines of North American novels.

I listened as they described shimmying down the Kurfestendam, pretending they could buy the glittering jewellery and soft clinging dresses that were in the brightly lit shop-windows. They would tell tales of their early days in England, often working as domestic servants for English Jewish people. They laughed at their own terrible English and the mistakes they made. The conversation invariably turned to emigration. It's always the transition points where our lives change that remain etched in our memory.

They remembered the discussions about where they could go, who could they write to, which country would let them in. I sat watching them at the table in front of our coal-fire. I was picking cake crumbs off the table with my finger. The names of loved ones left behind lingered on their lips, half-whispered in the air. Sometimes I would ask where they were now, or in which country did they end up. The answer would be the same.

"I don't know, *verschollen*, she just disappeared." There would be a short silence, only the sound of the knitting needles, then a new conversation would start up again in German, noisy, bright laughter, jokes, casting on new stitches, always new stitches.

The choreography of knitting

> *...the number one reason knitters knit is because...*
> *they need knitting to make boring things interesting....*
> *they simply can't tolerate boredom. It takes more to*
> *engage and entertain this kind of human, and they*
> *need an outlet or they get into trouble.......they just*
> *can't sit waiting at the doctor's office.*
> Stephanie Pearl-McPhee

Knitting is a dance between hands, yarn and needles. There is a myriad of different stitches to creates infinite patterns, flat, raised, lacy, ribbed, yarn in front, yarn behind, double yarn over the needle-slipped stitches, stitches passed over. Garter stitch looks the same on both sides; stocking stitch has a right side and a wrong side (RS and WS), a knit row and a purl row. I was reluctant to move on from garter stitch because knitting rows felt easy and I could zip along. Purling was slower and needed more effort. I made my grandmother an egg cosy in stocking stitch, two colours in a checked pattern.

The skeins of wool are bought at Leeds Kirkgate market. Sometimes Uncle Harry bought a job lot very cheap from Heckmondwike, newly dyed. These were all laid out on the kitchen table. They're counted and measured and colour compared to check they were dyed in the same batch. If variations appeared, the odd ball would be used for cuffs or a welt, the edging for the cardigan, the rim of a hat, the thumb of a mitten. Then we all sit in pairs, one holding arms apart and the other winding the skeins into balls. The room is full of winding and holding, weaving over and under. The finished balls are tossed into the waiting holdalls and casting on commences.

My refugee aunties were calmed by the repetition of the stitches, the monotony of the pattern, the comforting to and fro of the needles. The knitting begins, a first row knitting into the back of the stitch to make the edge of the garment firm. Leni has already lost a stitch.

Granny's knitting is tight, even and confident. She used bright colours and plain patterns with multi-coloured trimming. When she had finished her sweaters, she would look at the collar and say:

"Let's draw a thread through with pompoms on the end."

I chose colours for the pompoms. She cut two circles of card out of her old white Senior Service cigarette packets with a sailor's face framed by a white life belt on the front. We wound the wool through them. I then helped make a cord by twisting threads together, later the extra bits would turn into hair ribbons for my dolls and ear ribbons for my teddies.

My Mum sculpted a garment, adapting the shape, combining and recombining sleeves, collar and darts, checking the decreasing or increasing lines of the pattern. She held a disembodied knitted sleeve over my arm and knew at a glance if it needed a row or two more. It was cheaper to knit and sew, whilst clothes were still rationed.

I was allowed to choose my mum's project, for summer and for winter, the excitement of deciding one's own colours and not having to stay with the picture on the pattern. Sometimes my mum would suggest different sleeves or a wider welt, or cuffs. I was entranced by the shaping, changing and adapting. These special garments were mine. The homemade garments were the coveted presents. The birthday present carefully ironed and wrapped, the new, perfect knitting.

Aunty Frieda's hands were red from plunging into warm washing up water. She knitted mittens for me that were attached to a tape through the sleeves of my coat. She also knitted socks, scarves and sleeveless striped pullovers to send to Lucy's grandchildren in Israel. She caught the tram down to Marks and Spencers on Briggate to buy pants and vests and little white short-sleeved shirts for the children. She begged a box from the grocer to wrap into a big parcel. She tied it up with string she had saved, fastening the knot with sealing wax. Every Hanukah a small parcel arrived from Lucy in Israel with three pieces of crochet such as a handkerchief, a tray cloth, or a small lacy doily for her siblings.

Beattie arrived with her knitting, smiling and waving from the gate. She wore thick brown Lisle stockings to cover her varicose veins. She was very short and as round as her small gold-rimmed spectacles. She limped slightly, holding her stick, in her shabby dark brown coat smelling of mothballs. She settled down in the armchair by the fire and started knitting.

She knitted large shawls, in moss stitch, nobbles and bobbles, rib and even Arran, which she wore fastened with a long narrow marcasite brooch, inset with pearls. It had belonged to her mother, she told me. It was the only thing she could bring with her.

Zerta Blumenkopf - Mrs Flowers on her Head - bent down and kissed me. I would inhale with half-closed eyes, breathing in the Imperial Leather smell of her arms. I was entranced by her jingle-jangle gold charm bracelet and have worn the gold piggy she gave me on my own wrist for many years. I'd catch a fleeting glimpse of bosom and lace as I succumbed to her embrace. Sometimes I'd follow her upstairs and watch her adjust the substantial upholstery of her elasticated flesh-coloured undergarments, loosening them to be more comfortable. She would collapse on the sofa, squishing the plush velvety cushion next to her and I would wriggle up like a puppy, pleased to stay close. She'd whip out her compact and the whiff of pressed pink powder made me sneeze. She applied a fresh thick layer of lipstick, the same blood red as her fingernails.

She came from Vienna, had taken English lessons in preparation for immigration and was the only one able to construct recognisable English sentences. She had an extensive vocabulary and addressed me in English, although much of our communication was non-verbal, hugs, kisses and me stroking her ocelot coat with the large shawl collar, pretending it was a pet dog.

Zerta had married after the war, an older man. Everyone referred to him as English, which meant 'not Jewish', a goy! I knew that because at Christmas we visited their flat. The room would be in darkness when we arrived and she'd lift me up as we came in so my eyes could take in the feast of twinkling lights, sparkly tinsel on the enormous Christmas tree. My father would not allow us to have a tree.

Zerta always knitted fancy lacy patterns, mainly in creamy caramel coffee colours, often threaded through with a metallic gold thread. If her garment was reaching completion she would open her large carpet bag and pull out packets of sequins or gold stars or rickrack wavy braid in iridescent bronze, scarlet, gold or turquoise. Her pins were held carefully between her lips whilst she attached the embellishments as edging round the neckline, round the sleeves and sometimes on the welt. She'd sew random sequins or stars across the bosom of the sweater. If on completion she thought it was all too plain she'd pull out a crochet hook and coloured sparkling yarn to crochet an entire collar onto the round neck, a rainbow transformation which I kept touching, tracing the newly formed patterns with my finger.

She gave me the left-over snippets of braid and beads. I added these to my Elastoplast tin of diamonds, tucked away in the sideboard drawer for a rainy day.

Zerta couldn't join in the conversation whilst she had pins in her mouth but nodded or shook her head vigorously so that the others would know she was listening. Sometimes silent tears would roll down her cheeks and she'd dab her eyes with her knitting until the yarn was sodden. Whenever she appeared wearing one of her beautiful jumpers I would think they were made of salt and sequins.

Leni Streuselhoffer was short and stumpy with wisps of grey hair escaping from a bun at the nape of her neck, a woollen headscarf knotted under one of her chins. She wore a tweed skirt and jacket with padded shoulders, her solid legs in thick wool stockings where the darning stitches were clearly visible. She wore sensible oxblood brogues, her feet turned out at 90 degrees when she walked.

"Verdamte Füsse, damn feet," she would complain, easing them out of her shoes before taking her knitting needles out of the bag. Sometimes her feet were puffy and swollen, she'd remove her stockings. Frieda brought an enamel bowl filled with hot water, infused with ginger. Leni would slowly lower her feet into the bowl with a sigh of relief. "Chilblains," granny said afterwards when I asked about the red marks on Leni's toes. Of course we all had chilblains in winter. The weather was freezing and we washed in icy bathrooms and often leapt into bed still wearing our vests and socks.

She made jumpers with ribbed waistlines and puffed 1940 sleeves reaching just above the elbow, two ends tying in a bow at the neck. She'd knit ochre, indigo and burnt orange, often using flecked wool so that other colours would magically appear as her knitting grew.

"*Bunt*" she exclaimed, that marvellous German word meaning multi-coloured, patterned, bright…. "*alles muss bunt sein*" everything must be full of colour.

She made many mistakes, because she would be concentrating more on the conversation. Granny would patiently pick up her dropped stitches, unravel the uneven rows and knit them up for her again.

Lottie Weiss hurried to the door with little steps in her high heels, with matching gloves, scarf and handbag. She wore nylons with a seam up the back. Her small hat was, fashioned out of feathers, held in place by a jewelled hatpin, which she removed carefully. She arranged her blonde curls in the hallway mirror, lifted her straight skirt to fix a pink metal suspender that had worked loose, before kissing everyone, commenting on the smell of the coffee, how nice my hair looked and squeezed into the chair beside the radio in the corner, beneath the stern gaze of great grandmother Calman.

Lotte said little, but in the silences between letters I sometimes heard her whisper '*verdamte verbrecher*', *(damned destroyers)*. She was quick to criticise Leni's dropped stitches or uneven rows of stocking stitch. She only knitted for herself, subdued colours in expensive cashmere wool sent from London. They were tessellated patterns knitted on fine needles and she frowned with concentration to get them right.

My father's Aunty Martha arrived late. He collected her from the train station. In Berlin she had worked as the secretary to Ernst Chain, co-recipient of the 1945 Nobel Prize for his work on penicillin. Now she worked in the refugee office that processed claims for restitution money.

She wore a straight, cotton dress in summer and a woollen one in winter with peep toe shoes or black over-galoshes, from

Berlin, and a handbag to match. I could hear them laughing long before the knock on the door. I flew to open it, hug her as she came through and waited to hear her comments on how I had grown, measuring me against her waist, elbow and as time passed her shoulder.

Martha sewed whilst the others knitted. I watched her apply eye shadow and blot her lipstick on the edge of her hankie. She changed her dress after the five-hour train journey from London. She was wearing silk cami-knickers, edged with lace. She'd sewn them herself, she told me, all by hand.

I wanted my doll to wear a white bride's dress with a long veil. "Easy,'" said Auntie Martha. "I'm staying for a week. We'll do it together." As we approached the haberdashery counter I was explaining I wanted the headdress fixed with flowers on either side with pearls. Martha didn't know the words in English for pearls, bits of white lace, tiny flowers, so I translated. We chose everything including a pack of needles and white cotton. She gave me stork-shaped scissors. She asked me to thread the needle for her. She turned my doll into a princess, carefully pinning the dress together and showing me how to stitch it. I sewed, listening to the women all chattering together, the laughter, their jokes, clothes, nail varnish, the springtime, pink blossom on the hawthorn tree outside the window. Other times, I sat on a stool at my grandmother's feet either drawing or playing cat's cradle with an aunty who happened to have a free pair of hands.

Aunties were women who went to a lingerie-maker and had bought their substantial bras and girdles made to measure, tight elasticised flesh-coloured fabric, broad serviceable satin straps. The female form was held firmly in place. The female form was beautiful, to be adorned, the face, as beautiful as possible, the hair lustrous, shiny, perfect, permed.

Yearnings for the familiarity of the motherland which had betrayed them faded as the years unravelled; new homes and relationships replaced those left behind. Their faces changed but shadows and wrinkles never dimmed their bright smiles, their glittering eyes helped along with a dab of powder and a slick of bright red lipstick. They refused to submit to clothes in subdued colours, the smell of boiled cabbage and freezing winters with thick yellow smog and grime from the coal burning in the grate.

The clothes they made for me as I grew older were never quite right, they also belonged to another era. This was at odds with the feminists who worked so hard to hide their female attributes, striding out in dungarees and shaved heads. I was weaned on sparkle and lace – and although I tried, never completely made the transition.

Tongues chattering, needles clattering, these émigré women warriors knitted and stitched a sequinned path into my heart. Their foreign accents still travel with me.

***

My own pursuit of Englishness was not always straightforward. They taught us knitting in school, the English way. Everyone was to bring grey wool and begin at the beginning by casting on in slow motion. My mum was unimpressed by the grey wool. She offered me pink or neon turquoise. I longed to accept but already had an impending sense of doom.

My mum knitted rainbow colours. She and my gran were creators of skirts with pink scalloped edging and fluffy striped jumpers. The women in my family held the needles close together whizzing along rows creating my new clothes. They created my precious royal blue pixie-hood and scarf, festooned with wild multi-coloured pom-poms. Sometimes they embroidered delicate woollen flowers on my cardigans. I would stand on the table as together they measured the length of knitted dresses with zigzag borders. I stretched out my arms so they could attach the sleeves, one holding the pins in her mouth, the other keeping my arm straight, gossiping away, cakes and continental coloured knitting, the only grey was our English winter drizzling outside the window.

"No, no it has to be grey like everyone else," I insisted. "I mustn't be different. I must be ready to start casting on."

We practised together that evening. She looped bright pink wool around her fingers, quickly accumulating stitches on the needle in her other hand. We counted together and soon I had pink stitches on my needle too. Meanwhile she unpicked the grey wool from an old sock of my dad's for school and I eagerly awaited the knitting class.

Miss Shawcross, asked if anyone had cast on before and I confidently raised my hand. She invited me to demonstrate. I had hardly begun looping grey wool around my fingers before she smacked them shouting, "No, no, you use needles, two needles. Go back to your place, till you can do it correctly." I returned to my desk eyes lowered, fighting tears.

Although my mum cheerfully continued to show me how to hold the yarn over my fingers and knit along the row, I sank to the bottom of the class as my dropped stitches sank to the bottom of my knitting. I forgot everything. I just stopped being able to knit.

A pair of giant needles lay on the teacher's desk with a square piece of plain knitting in lime green string. Every time one of us dropped a stitch we had to stand in front of the class and knit a row of lime green. After the casting on debacle it was usually me standing there. Six years old, grubby socks, one up, one down. I worked the needles painfully, attempting to reach the end of the row with all my stitches intact. At the end of term the teacher presented me with the green object.

"A dishcloth," she said. "You've done most of it, take it home to show your Mother."

I walked disconsolately out of school, tearing the lime green yarn with my teeth, but it was stringy and hard. I slipped into a shaded driveway and dug into a stranger's flowerbed with my bare hands, burying the shameful object. My mother was a Rainbow knitter; I couldn't reveal the secret of my failed endeavour.

2009

My Mum is ninety. One day we go on an outing to the seaside. I drive to Whitby. There is a church hall that sells miscellaneous bric-a-brac. We walk up there, as we have done for years, after being blown away on the beach, dwarfed by crashing waves. We walk up the hill, very slowly, eating fish and chips. She sits on the wall for a rest, complaining "not enough vinegar."

We make a beeline for the knitting stand. My mother, ever practical, would be examining sturdy garments, tightly knitted, inquire about the ability of different wools to withstand washing, calculate how many balls she would need for the next cardigan. Meanwhile I would be mesmerised by ethereal shawls in delicate pastel colours, cobweb patterns as if knitted by fairies. If I could knit a shawl like that would it be in pale blue wash or pale pink to fuchsia weaving gold threads through, or I would make a shawl the colours of the sea, from grey to green?

I tell her about the new knitting movement. Knit and bitch groups of young women sit on sofas in smart bars clicketting, clattering, knitting and chattering away. She senses a wistfulness in my tale and buys me balls of the sea green wool. We are going to try again and begin together. She still swiftly winds the yarn under and over arthritic fingers. She waits for me to catch up. I copy, we count together and soon I have multi-coloured stitches on my needle. I can do this! On the train home I practice over and under and marvel at the fabric growing on the needle. However, when the pattern instructs "incl, p 2 tog", I'm lost. A stitch drops so I visit the local knitting shop for help. The lady's nostrils flare, "You've made a mess." She unravels the mess and my years unravel back to the shame of my childhood.

"The casting on is wrong." It can't be, my mum knew exactly how to magic stitches on to the needle. "Start again." I leave the shop, tears prickling.

I sit in front of my laptop and search for knitting videos on YouTube. Round the world women teach casting on in different languages. They progress to the dancing needles and jacquard patterns of my knitting dreams. I search for German knitting. Flying fingers appear before my very eyes, casting on just like my mum. The yarn is on the left side.

The internet revealed that after the war German knitting became unpopular. Maybe my teacher long ago noticed I had been learning to knit like the enemy. Maybe she had no idea I was surrounded by rainbow jumpers made with yarn held on the left. The German knitters in my home were oblivious that, in the outside world, knitters were holding their yarn on the right side.

Now I cast on proudly, a continental knitter, my yarn confidently held on the left, as the women in my family did before me. I have earned my rightful place on the knit and bitch sofas, in the new multicultural millennium of English knitters.

1953

I have always bought cheap white IKEA furniture, relieved not to be oppressed by the dark German wood, polished by Granny and Frieda; all purchased by Eugene Weiss, under orders by the Nazis to spend all his German money prior to departure. Consequently, my grandmother's living room was dominated by a huge, black sideboard carved with ornate cherubs, birds and fruit. It contained twenty-two volumes of Meyer's lexicon; this was an old German encyclopaedia. I used to take out a volume, poring over the black ink drawings of wild flowers with their names written in Latin and German. There were also colour plates of painted birds separated by thin leaves of tissue.

The top drawer held old family photos, papers, my grandmother's favourite sweets, aniseed balls, spare knitting needles and some balls of wool. The next drawer had her writing paper, fountain pen and a bottle of green Quink ink. I reach into the top drawer for a sixpenny bar of chocolate. I can tell the flavour by the colour: pink was strawberry, green mint, dark blue fruit and nut. The chocolate waits for me every Wednesday afternoon with my comic, Girl. It is glossy, shiny with inviting colour cartoons stories about adventures in an all girls' boarding school and, on the back page, the story of a heroic woman from history. Ruth from the Old Testament cared for her mother-in-law Naomi after her husband Boaz died, Florence Nightingale, the lady with the lamp, and drawings of soldiers lying on the floor on bloodied mattresses, various missionaries from Africa and Violette Szabo, resistance fighter. I read these stories carefully munching on squares of strawberry chocolate. The luxury of reading and escaping, to a magic world, weaving dreams from other worlds.

There were cartoon recipes. Aunty Frieda and I would often make them together. I'd translate the ingredients into German for her and we would often spend a long time converting grams into ounces and litres into pints. We beat ingredients with a wooden spoon until our arms ached. She opened her 'saved paper' drawer, full of wrappings from shopping, tiny bits of silver paper, sweet wrappers meticulously smoothed out. She brought out a leftover piece of greaseproof paper, cheese wrapping from the grocer's, smoothed it out and wiped it clean. We rubbed it with a morsel of fat and then lined a baking tin. After our session, if possible, it would be cleaned again, folded and placed back in the drawer, sometimes I would beg her to let me use it to trace a favourite picture from my comic.

The *Girl* recipes included chocolate cornflakes, melting chocolate and margarine (there was still post-war rationing, coupons and ration books) together in a pan and then shaking in cornflakes, hoping it would all stick together. Once we made Baked Alaska, using a block of three-coloured Neapolitan ice cream, beating egg whites with sugar from a brown packet and using it to cover the ice cream. The egg whites glistened golden and hot but the ice cream stayed cold; it all melted in the mouth at the same time.

We washed the pots together while listening to the afternoon play on the radio; everything always stayed the same.

News from overseas

There were special Sunday afternoons once a month at my Gran's for the reading of letters accompanied by coffee and special cakes. Everyone dressed up as though we were going to greet the letter writers in person. Ample backsides sank into the squishy cushions of my Gran's red velvet sofa.

Letters ... they had already been pored over in the different households and were now going to be read aloud in German, within the circle of the extended family, connecting us around the world. They came from the US, South Africa, Israel, Chile, Switzerland and Peru, in tight German script.

I learnt about the extended family. There were names attached to countries across the seas, beyond the horizon and inaccessible in the fifties, unless you saved up for years to make one trip.

Aunties would rummage in their handbags and reach for spectacles or magnifying glasses then unfold the tissue - thin blue sheets of airmail paper. Each aunty read a letter in turn.

Lucy's - letters from Israel - describing the dusty town of Ramat Hasharon, the terrible heat. She sends monochrome pictures with scalloped edges of her two grandchildren, a boy and girl (like us), wearing identical white shorts, squinting at the camera in bright sunlight. She missed the cold in Berlin and the times they all went ice-skating together..

Harry's from Chile, - Beattie's grandson - his letters were brief, in stilted English that he was learning in school. He described his favourite subjects, the rain, how he enjoyed climbing. Beattie smiled as she folded his letters carefully placing them back in her handbag.

My blind grandmother's - from South Africa – she writes in spidery German *Sütterling schrift* that formed the bridge between Gothic upright traditional writing and a modern looser script. It loops and curls over the thick, grooved Braille paper. She sometimes sends parcels of crystallised fruits. She once sent a pink glass heart on a silver chain, which I kept round my neck even in the bath, always special kisses for Johnny and me, immediately delivered by the reader.

My grandmother's friend, Frau Hausner, wrote from Lausanne, Switzerland. She once visited with a feathered hat and a strange accent when she spoke German. My aunt's aunt, Ella, lived in Munchen Gladbach, Germany, and we made a day trip to Scarborough when she visited. She held me on a donkey so that I wouldn't fall off as it trotted along. She kept kissing me and I was mesmerised by the carved elephants on her jade pendant. I asked her if there were elephants where she lived, confused at this conglomerate of countries and which were hot which were cold, where the elephants lived and where Jews had hidden in forests to survive.

Betty, I'm not sure whose cousin, in America, tells us the price of coffee, and nylon stockings and asks if we still need food parcels, offering to send more tins of condensed milk. I hope another parcel might be on the way. Last time she sent me a silver swimming costume decorated with pictures of the planets. It was a bit big but my mum said no one would notice in the sea.

The sisters, Margarete and Frieda, baked for two days before the letter readings at their house. I'd sit on a stool in the kitchen and sift icing sugar over the hazelnut cake. I'd sprinkle the streusel, a crumbly mix of sugar, flour and butter over the plum cake before it went into the oven and then sit waiting, reading my comic in the warm kitchen, breathing in the sugary buttery smells. When the cakes had come out of the oven and were cooling safely on their wire trays my grandmother changed into her afternoon clothes. She wore a blouse with a pussy bow; her cardigan and straight skirt were plain grey. No one ever wore trousers, not even me. This was the 1950s, everything was neat, ordered and respectable.

My granny's Art Nouveau dressing table has travelled through the decades of my life. I look in the centre of the triptych mirror and still see her sitting patiently pinning up her hair with delicate wire pins; they never held my thick plaits in place. Only now I realise that her hair had become gossamer fine with age and she kept it long because when pinned up there seemed more of it. I'd curl the little white wisps at the nape of her neck round my finger, made giddy by her perfume and watching her dangly earrings sway every time her head dipped to reach for another pin. I would play with my own hair in the side mirror, sitting on a little stool she'd brought up from the kitchen. I held her earring against my face and shook it. Sometimes we'd catch each other's eye and start pulling faces, seeing who could pull the ugliest face without laughing. She always won.

I picked flowers from the garden to put on the table. Or I made a daisy chain and arranged it in a pattern on the tablecloth or I surprised my grandmother by putting daisies and buttercups in little eggcups and arranging them around the living room.

***

The cut glass, kept in the Jacobean sideboard, was only used on special occasions, such as letter reading afternoons. There was an oval dish with bobbles cut into the glass and two stars whose seven sharp points splintered the light into rainbows. My responsibility was to carry the cut glass, one piece at a time, from the cupboard to the kitchen where my great aunt submerged each piece in soapy water and polished it until it sparkled like diamonds. The cut glass had come from Germany, carefully wrapped up in pieces of duster, piled up in the lift my grandmother had described.

I was always told, "Look after the cut glass (Krystal in German), it'll be worth a fortune one day." It was carried carefully from house to house through the generations. "Be careful with the cut glass," my mother said, shortly before she died.

I was always being told to be careful, to be very careful. I was a child who dropped the jam pot as I stuck my finger in it, who almost stabbed herself as she jabbed at the plastic lid of the butter box to open it quickly.

My childhood is speckled with the tiny shards of cut glass.

I was carrying a tray very slowly...I broke goblets, dessert meringue plates, small dishes; they fell to the floor with a smash. Pieces of glass scattered everywhere. Everything went silent, no one spoke. I bent down to start picking up the pieces; I knew I'd done something terrible, hot tears on my cheeks. A grown up said, "No, leave it, I'll do it, you'll only cut yourself."

Inevitably I already had, blood running down the side of my hand on to my dress, drips on to my white socks, drops fell on small pieces of broken glass glittering on the floor. They all stood looking down at the bits of glass spattered with droplets of my blood. My granny held my hand under the cold water tap and then tied her hanky round the cut.

"It's Krystal," I said proud of my German. "Broken glass, it's the night of broken glass. It's Krystallnacht."

Silence.

I never felt at ease with this cut glass; I felt burdened by it. I never understood why we should keep something that could break so easily. I felt a responsibility associated with a meaning that eluded me. Within a week of my mother's death I transported it to the auction house. I watched uneasily as my granny's crystal was being unwrapped by strangers. I received £80 – this was the family fortune, this was what was going to set them up in England. Hitler took their livelihoods, their money, their houses, but the cut glass would see them through. They could never part with it, they always held on to it for the next generation.

Johnny and Carry

Mama Gornitzky and Granny Weiss

Chapter 8

In summer our supper would be cold cherry or gooseberry soup, served with a large chunk of rye bread.

"Johnny, what's mum doing?"

"She's watching next door. They're packing their car."

"Where are they going?"

"Dunno, holiday."

My Mum watches the neighbours' car disappear down the street. She waits another fifteen minutes to make sure they don't return, then she gives me a basket and helps us both over the fence into their garden. She passes a ladder over and joins us with another basket.

"What are we doing?" I ask. Johnny as usual seems to know and is leaning the ladder against the trunk.

"We're picking cherries."

"We could buy some."

"It's not the same, besides these are special cherries. Morello cherries, you can't often get them in England".

I have to climb the tree because I'm the smallest and can get to the highest branches. I taste one.

"Ugh, mum they're too sour, I'm coming down."

"You stay up there till the baskets full.

"What? In chicken soup?"

"No, a special cold soup, with sour cream, I'll make it tomorrow. And jam."

We picked until there were only a few left right at the top of the tree.

"For the birds," said my mum.

"Suppose they come back early and find we've picked all their cherries," I say as Johnny helps me down the ladder.

I have black juice all round my mouth, it dribbles down my dress, and a slight tummy ache.

"They won't, they'll think the birds ate them all."

She was excited; she had a basket full of Morello cherries to make jam, just like in Germany.

Visitors from Israel

Distant cousins arrived from Israel, tall and blond with open-necked shirts, khaki shorts, contemptuous of our suburban English lifestyle. They sat on the grass looking with disapproval at my mother's lovingly tended herbaceous borders. She spent long Saturday afternoons gardening. I worked alongside as she staked the drooping lupins. Together we built wigwams out of twigs and garden canes to support pastel coloured sweet peas.

English summer, soft, light drizzle never far away and the smell of freshly cut grass. "Look," she would say, producing some bulbs wrapped in newspaper out of her pinny pocket. "These are autumn crocuses, if we plant them now, in the grass, we'll discover surprise flowers in October." I waited eagerly for the papery violet petals to peep out of the green grass in the last sunshine before winter.

The Israeli cousins told us we should be planting trees, helping to build the state of Israel and when we grew older we should help build the country, it depended on us.

The State of Israel was founded in 1948. The little blue and white tin was placed on the shelf by the front door. I used to sit on the bottom step watching visitors put a few coins in the slot at the top. It was about ten inches high with a picture of a tree, a Star of David and some Hebrew writing. In Yiddish the tin was called a "Pushke", the blue box initiated the Jewish National Fund as early as 1882. Israel referred to Eretz Israel, a relationship with the land, communities, agriculture, roads, water, reservoirs. It connected Jews in the Diaspora with Israel, *making the desert bloom.*

Johnny and I often used to try ransacking the tin, shaking it so the coins clunked inside, pennies, threepenny bits, small silver sixpences and the occasional half-crown. We discussed how our contribution wouldn't really make a difference to building the new country. I asked my Father why we didn't live in Israel. He answered that he didn't really believe it was our country - we had taken it from the Arabs, just as our homes had been taken by the Nazis, and eventually we must find a way of sharing it as we did thousands of years ago.

"Why do Jewish people need a homeland?" I asked.

"To be safe," he answered.

"Jews who were robbed of their homes needed somewhere to live," answered my Mum. "The few who survived were in displacement camps at the end of the war and then ended up all over the world."

"We were always moving, even before the war," remarked my father. "We were often never allowed to settle."

We're settled now," said my mum. "We know where we belong."

My dad was silent.

"So where do we really come from?" I needed to know. My parents both answered at the same moment.

"On my side Russia, Poland," my Dad said.

"LEEDS," said my mum emphatically. "You're Yorkshire through and through."

"That depends how far back you want to go. On your mother's side Morocco, which is why she has red hair, then her family travelled through Spain, France and finally ended up in southern Germany."

Thea glares at Manfred. She doesn't like this description of uncertainties about our origins; she wants to know who we all are, where we live, everything must stay the same forever.

"You were born in Leeds like I was born in Dewsbury, that's where we're from, this is where we belong." She closes the conversation.

I climb on my father's knee. He had turned up the volume on the radio, another concert broadcast on the BBC third programme. The violins struck up the overture. I wound the tassel on my cardigan round my finger, puzzling the question of our homeland, My neat little black plaits tied at the top of my head with a huge pink bow didn't make me look like I was Leedsish, in fact I looked like the girl in the drawing of the German Twins in my book, except my hair is dark. Also, my father had a funny name.

Again I knew not to push the conversation further. Maybe I could return to it sometime later. I slid down from his knee and slipped out of the room to interrupt my brother. He was lying on the floor of his room working out cricket scores.

"Where do we come from?"

"Inside our mum's tummy."

"Does that make us Leedsish?"

"You can't be, Leedsish"

"Yorkshire- ish?"

"British fathead." Even more confusing. English, I might have understood.

"Can I say made in Leeds then, Pig face?"

"Yep," he rolled his little metal score keeper, he'd lost interest.

"Can I play?"

"Nope."

"Please."

He hesitated. "If you hand over next week's pocket money."

"OK"

***

Sixpence pocket money per week, home-made chocolates from Ackerman in mum's sideboard, locked and the key out of reach.

Struggling to play two balls against the red brick wall of granny's house, dress tucked into knickers in case I managed to throw the ball under one leg and catch it against the wall.

Clarks' sandals fitted in a machine that showed an x-ray of your foot and you had to wiggle you toes to check there was lots of room to grow. One pair of sandals per year and a pair of black lace ups, which I could never tie, for winter, another pair for best with a bar strap and button which I could never fasten and then wellies for trailing through puddles, cold feet but clean socks.

Hopscotch on granny's paved driveway, and a whip and top in a toy cupboard, sitting on the pavement drawing chalk pictures, packets of chalk with pocket money and a metal spinning top in many colours making a humming noise as it twirled round the kitchen on the lino.

Winter meant no bruised ankles playing dreadful hockey but magnificent Greek dancing, wearing lime green tunics in silky material, cold against the skin if not warmed on the pipes in the changing room. We danced the story of Pluto in the underworld to Grieg's Peer Gynt and we all leapt about ferociously to Hall of the Mountain King, being wicked creatures of the underworld.

Television

Every Tuesday afternoon, I watched an episode of the Rose and the Ring, a serialised drama for children on TV. I bought the theme music, Swedish Rhapsody, with my pocket money and played it on the wind-up dark green gramophone from my mother's childhood, a chrome arm with a speaker on the end. The needle needed changing after playing two or three of the 78s.

The wood veneer television cabinet stood in front of the bay window with leaded panes and thick, lined velvet curtains in green, black and ochre stripes. At 5pm Gran would open the two doors ceremoniously for us to watch a special programme. The rounded screen filled the top half and underneath was the speaker and knobs that I was forbidden to touch. There was only one channel, the BBC, which broadcast after 5pm. A sign appeared on the screen saying intermission. A short film, with gentle music in the background, was shown between programmes. There was a kitten playing with a ball of string, a potter's hands on the wheel modelling wet clay into a vase, waves breaking on a seashore. Everything was in fuzzy black and white.

Whilst my granny and great aunt were drinking a cup of tea, I was allowed to watch children's programmes. *Muffin the Mule* was a marionette horse, hooves clattering in a clumsy Morris dance. He danced on top of a piano. Annette Mills, a lady in a tight perm wearing pearls, played the piano as she sang.

Here comes Muffin, Muffin the Mule,
Here comes Muffin playing the fool,

Annette Mills also presented Prudence Kitten, a glove puppet dressed in sprigged chintz dresses. She often clutched a duster and complained about the mess in the house. Primrose, her sister, had a sailor husband called Nelson whose friend was a dog called Puffer. The boy animal got up to mischief, the girl did housework.

My parent's wedding movie

I'm eight years old, staring at a white sheet pinned to our living room wall. I'm sitting in darkness, watching grainy black and white film. My dad is the projectionist.

A single shaft of light projects the flickering images of my parents' wedding. The only sound is the whirring of spools turning on the 8mm movie projector. The characters on the sheet are laughing, hands holding wine glasses, arms raised, toasting and, by the way their lips are moving, often singing.

There are only a few shots of my teenage mother, the bride with flowers in her hair. She waves shyly with one hand, the other holding her long shiny dress, nervous she'll trip on her stiletto heels. There are many shots of my dad, Jack the Lad, aged 24, dark eyes flashing, kissing his bride, kissing his mother, pushing and shoving his younger brother, and lunging forward to grab the camera.

I'm noticing another figure always somewhere in shot. He also looks about 24. He is laughing, he plays camera tag with my Dad; one films a few seconds, then the other one. They film each other. He pulls faces at the camera, he makes my dad pull faces, he kisses the bride, then the bridesmaid, once, twice

"Who's he?" I ask.

"My best man, Manfred Marks."

"He's funny."

"He was."

"Has he visited us?"

"No."

"Why not?"

No answer.

"Why not, Daddy?"

No answer.

"Where is he?"

Pause

"He just disappeared."

What did that mean? How can you just disappear? I think of the pot labelled vanishing cream on my mum's dressing table. Did he apply it and then pouf, he disappeared? Was it a joke? Has he disappeared forever? Silence, except for the whirring of the spools.

I glance back to the screen, my Dad and his best man are now dancing together, a Russian dance, going down on their haunches, kicking their legs and falling over each other helpless with laughter.

"How did he disappear?"

Silence except for the whirr of the projector.

"Is he your best friend, Manfred Marks?"

"Yes, he was. We were at school together, we were always in trouble with the teacher, he called us Manfred one and two."

"Which were you?"

"Manfred two, I was the younger."

"If he is your best friend why doesn't he write to you?"

I understand about writing letters. Every month I listen to the letters read out by my Gran and great aunts. So why didn't he write?

Just the whirring of the spools.

I watch Manfred One on the film blow kisses at the camera. I watch Manfred Two stare frozen at the screen. I really wanted to know what happened, but I daren't ask any more. A fog of silence had descended.

A long pause, everyone kissing everyone else on the screen. Eventually, I tried again.

"Daddy...."

"Yes?"

"How can you just disappear?"

He turns to me in the dark. I scrutinise his face, lit up by the projector beam. For a moment I felt scared, I thought he was angry with me, I knew what happened if I went too far, I moved carefully away from him, silently out of reach of his hand, just in case. He held my gaze for a long time.

"His Mum said they came at dawn, there was a knock on the door and they took him away, we never heard again."

I shift slightly in my seat and pull my socks up.

"Did they come at dawn for you?"

"I had already left. We left straight after the wedding."

I turn back to the screen. My parents are running along a station platform each carrying a large, stiff leather suitcase. Manfred Marks is leading a gaggle of waving, leaping young people throwing confetti. The images wobble as the camera is passed around. The next shots are from the train; my father is filming his friends. There is a long close-up of Manfred Marks' face and his eyes seem to meet mine in our darkened 1950s living room. Then the screen goes black. The whirring has stopped.

We sit in silence for what seems forever. I suck the ends of my pigtails.

"Daddy, who are all those people throwing confetti?"

"Friends."

"Where are they now?"

"They just disappeared."

Where did they go, I wonder, where did they go?

***

After school I hurried home to be cosily inside before dark. It was school black lace-up shoes off, slippers on. Then it was a warm cup of tea on a blowy winter's day and a piece of cake before going upstairs for homework. A quiet house, alone with my imagination, school books on the desk and permission to lose myself inside my head and on the paper. I felt safe upstairs studying and reading and learning vocabulary, verb conjugations. I'd learn poems for fun because I liked the stillness up in my room above the 1950s kitchen with its Formica worktop and blue enamel stove. I'd listen to the pots in the sink and smell the cooking dinner.

My father drove home from the disused swimming pool in Bramley, the factory where he manufactured shampoo, soap and once strawberry bath essence. He gave Lotte, his friend, also from Berlin a bottle for her birthday. It dyed her whole body red and took six weeks to fade. He delivered his manufactured goods to chemists and household shops around the north of England. One half-term morning he bundled us into the back of the car, hardly able to contain his excitement. We thought we were visiting Mama and Papa but he drove past Manchester, on the road to Liverpool. He turned off at Burtonwood, an American Army base that placed regular orders for Gorney cleaning materials, Regency hair cream and strawberry Crème Shampoo (sometimes banana scented). He led us into the canteen. Our eyes were on stalks at the sumptuous ice-cream sundaes in tall glasses dripping with chocolate sprinkles and a coloured paper parasol. There was a galaxy of toppings and sauces and colours of ice cream. We sat on tall bar stools at the counter silently eating, licking chocolate off our lips and tasting each other's flavours. Even in Berlin my father had never eaten such wonderful ice-cream ; for Johnny and me it was the first taste of America, along with parcels of tinned food, jazz music on TV and black and white films of thirties musicals.

My next encounter with America would be a man in a full-length rabbit fur coat.

2014

I am watching a tall man walk towards me. For a moment I think it is Kurt but he died aged 92, an upright old Jew with a hybrid Berlin/Lancashire accent. During the Yom Kippur service, even as he became frail, he would insist on standing for long periods, in synagogue close to the Ark. Uncle Kurt and my Aunty Helga put down roots in Manchester. They found their community within their synagogue. Like many refugees they gave their children perfect English names, Ronnie and Susie.

Sometimes I get lost in between decades and fall into the cracks between the stories. It's my cousin Ronnie approaching the Hampstead café. He is limping, he has twisted his knee after some wild dancing the previous night. We sit in the sunshine drinking coffee. I watch him devour two eggs on toast, sad that we don't see each other more often. He is a committed religious Jew, son of Kurt. I am a secular atheist Jew, daughter of Manfred. I'm pleased to see him; he's wonderfully familiar.

"Do you remember Gornozan?" he asks suddenly. I shake my head.

"You must remember Gornozan, they used it for everything."

"When? In Berlin?"

"No, in Leeds…Manchester when we were little. Your father, Uncle Manfred, made it in his factory. They must have made it already in Berlin. My dad might have given him the recipe."

"What did they use it for?"

"If we cut ourselves …Gornozan, if we grazed a knee, Gornozan….if we had an infection Dad would make a Gornozan poultice, they used it as hair cream too."

"Always applied externally?"

Ronnie laughs. "Yes, it was used to clean surfaces, everything. Carry, it was a major part of my childhood."

"What happened when Manfred stopped manufacturing?" I asked, remembering my father's business was bankrupted sometime in the late fifties.

"My father was desperate, he didn't know how he would manage without it. When the factory closed, Uncle Manfred drove over the Pennines with his boot crammed full of Gornozan tins for Daddy. They lasted us another twenty five years."

I liked this picture of my Dad delivering Gornozan to my Uncle Kurt.

We wondered if the original Gornozan came before or after the kosher potato crisps.

Gillian Cohen

Gillian and I are playing at weddings. With ink-stained fingers she threads my mum's white petticoat through a plastic Alice band and places the veil on my head. I scrutinise the effect in the mirror. We are about to perform a wedding ritual together. My mum's dressing gown was my long dress and she was still in her navy school gymslip. I had carefully drawn her moustache with mum's eyeliner. She was playing two male roles, the bridegroom and an ill-defined figure who conducted the ceremony.

"With this ring I thee wed." She pulled a key ring, found in the playground, out of her pocket, It had traces of cold, school mashed potato that she had secreted there at lunch to avoid the teacher trying to force her to eat it. I had provided a decoy, distracting miss whilst Gillian shovelled the thick lumpy white mass into her pocket. She didn't want another rap with the ruler across her fingers.

"I promise to be good for ever," I say solemnly, eyeing my ring.

Gillian is scornful. "No, you have to be much more serious. This is a wedding, it's for life, like a dog."

I am now preoccupied with adding some of my mum's rouge to my cheeks. I turn to Gillian, the tiara (twisted raffia found in the neighbour's dustbin) falls over one eye. "What do I have to say?"

She intones in front of me, "you will not steal, you will cover your neighbour's ass and honour your husband." I recognised something biblical in her words. I had been forcing my mum's white patent court shoes over my school socks and now stood up. She was next to me now we looked in the mirror and both solemnly said at the same moment "I do."

Then we held hands and jumped up and down on my parents' bed until we collapsed giggling, sucking the remnants of the lemon sherbet which had also been secreted in her pocket, mixed with lumps of mashed potato.

Gillian Cohen and I had been friends since the infants. She was a year younger than me. We swore to go to the same secondary school. I had to go first and told her wild and terrible tales of my adventures there. Everyone called me Dusky, I lied. I also elaborated on my feats of courage, all based on a combination of the *Famous Five* and *What Katy Did* with some of the stories on the back of *Girl* magazine thrown in. Gillian's mother came over from Hamburg on the Kindertransport, aged fifteen. "I lost everyone," was her only comment about her German life.

Aunty Elsa was always anxious Gillian would be home on time, *punktlich*, as she would say in her Hamburg accent,. Gillian and I dawdled down the road from school trailing our satchels. "*Pünktlich* we have to be" she said, imitating her mother's accent. "*Pünktlich*" we chanted pushing each other into puddles, our cheeks bulging with massive aniseed balls bought for a penny at the shop on the corner.

"You watch," said Gillian, "when we turn the corner." She dropped all her belongings and stood, pointing exaggeratedly at her wrist. "Vot time is zis?" Point, point, jabbing her finger. We were laughing as we turned the corner. At the bottom of the hill was her block of flats where I could just make out the outline of her mother at the window. We ran down the hill, Gillian not really wanting to be late and I hopeful that there would be a slice of homemade chocolate and chopped hazelnut cake waiting for us.

Mushrooms grew on the bathroom wall. We helped each other to balance on the edge of the bath so we could feel their spongy heads. There was a Dansette record player and Elsa carefully placed the needle on one of Bill Haley's 78s. The three of us danced round the Formica kitchen table.

Sitting in their little kitchen sipping hot milky coffee, I suspected Elsa danced to records all day. I imagined her dancing round the house in her flat ballet pumps and pedal pushers. We all took it in turns to practise jiving and jitterbugging until exhausted we flopped on their living room three piece suite. Gillian and I ate more cake washed down with glasses of watery Ribena.

Gillian and I never mentioned the Germans to Aunty Elsa. Once I dared ask how she got here, by train and a big boat.

"I looked after twins on the way, babies, they were put in an old drawer not to fall out whilst the train was moving."

"Did babies come?" I was incredulous, knowing that babies belonged with their mam.

"Of course, children of all ages, many never saw their mums again, many didn't even remember them." Her eyes filled with tears, her mascara ran and I wished I'd never asked her.

My father was happy to meet with Germans. He called me to come over one night when he had a business guest from Germany. I came reluctantly, wearing dungarees and Doc Martins, with my wild hair and sunglasses, lolling in the armchair chewing gum. My father wore his suit, shook hands eagerly and played the man of the house. My mother had made a healthy meal, *Rindfleisch mit Kartoffel* and her special gravy.

I could hardly look into the man's eyes, let alone watch my father fawning over him. I was consumed with questions. What had this guy done in the war? What had his father done in the war? Would he be sitting at my parents' table if he knew what happened to my father in the war? Why was I sitting at the table with him? Had my father even told him we were Jewish? I left before pudding.

Journey through Europe

The best moment of the year for Manfred was when we were in the car, off on holiday. He wanted to sit in cafes with umbrellas, sipping his drink, watching Europeans. He longed to speak German and skirted round Germany and Austria, mainly visiting German-speaking parts of Switzerland. As soon as the engine was running and the car started to move he was euphoric. The journey started with rushing down to Dover. I packed a bag with treasures, a hair ribbon and a box of crayons and paper. I would create a den for my dolls in the back, carefully tucking them in with a blanket.

My father always insisted we both sat motionless in absolute silence when we approached any European border. He was always concerned with officialdom and that his papers would be in order. He was afraid he would make a mistake.

"*Die Papiere, die Papiere*" ("the papers, the papers,") he would hiss at my mother, as the guard approached our car with its GB plates. He'd panic about the passports at the "Grenze" (the border), sweat pouring off his face as the border guards stamped our passports. Maybe he was going to be interrogated and he would be found out.

Manfred orders another cup of coffee, "mit Sahne", (with cream). He remembers the glacier from when he travelled to Switzerland, with his Zionist youth group. They walked the glacier, singing Zionist songs and laughing. Now he had driven from Leeds in his little 1948 Morris, his children sitting in the back of the car giggling and whispering together.

"What did they talk about?" he often wondered, glancing at them in his rear view mirror. Occasionally he heard a German word and then more giggles.

Rubel Magda, Schmoozles, kernoodles, Wiltschwein, Sonnesnschein, Reise Ausfahrt, Uberfarht, Einfahrt .

We drove into Europe every summer, travelling onward whilst the money lasted. When there was just sufficient for the return to *Blighty*, he turned round, sometimes driving through the night. My Mum would sit at the back with us snuggled against her wrapped in blankets, I listened sleepily to the hum of the engine, my Mum telling us stories about driving just like this, from Dewsbury to Berlin, when she was little like me.

"Was Uncle Harry at the back like us?"

"No he was in boarding school."

"Were you lonely?"

"I had my doll, Nellie."

"And your pretend friends."

"Yes of course, Nitchymitch and Sand were always there."

Johnny snored. We were quiet, just the rain beating against the windscreen and the squeaking of the wipers. Granny, at the front, was dozing too. She'd awaken with a start, pour a cup of strong black coffee from a flask.

"Where are we Manfred?"

"Driving along the Rhine, we're just coming to the Lorelei rock."

"Then we'd better sing so she doesn't entice you off the road."

They both laughed and burst into song

Ich Weiss nicht was sol es bedeuten,
Dass ich so traurig bin;
Ein Marchen aus alten Zeiten,
Das kommt nicht aus dem Sinn
(I know not if there is a reason
Why I am so sad at heart
A legend of bygone ages
Haunts me and will not depart)

I lay dozing, listening to the words by Heinrich Heine, lulled to sleep by the fairy tale images.

Ihr goldenes Geschmeide blitzet
Sie kammt ihr goldenes Haar.
(Her golden jewels are shining,
She's combing her golden hair)

I asked my Gran about Heine. "Jewish," she said. "Well, he converted, but then I think he converted back. He was one of the Jewish non-Jews."

Yet again I was confused.

***

On Sunday mornings my father gave me flying lessons. This involved arduous effort because I never actually took off. My mother and brother used to lie in bed watching, whilst they ate eggs with soldiers. He would open the bedroom window and hold me under the tummy as if I were learning to swim. He held me outside the window and issued instructions.

"Fly, fly straight to Granny's house."

I flapped my arms obediently, straining to take off over the grey rooftops and smoking chimneys, reaching up towards the open sky. My father would check the route with me while I asked anxiously whether Granny would have her window open for me, how would I get back home and would there be time for a glass of squash and a piece of her chocolate cake?

We discussed the wind on my face and how it would blow my hair back, he reminded me about dodging birds. I wanted him to come with me; the two of us would be able to do it. Alone, I never took off and eventually we'd climb back into bed, and listen to Uncle Mac's Children's Favourites on the wireless. If I was lucky he would play "Sparky and the Magic Piano."

He would rustle his newspaper, contemplating the real world. I'd gaze out of the window at the sky, wondering how high the clouds were, wondering if I really took off would I fly so far away and never come back, wondering if pianos would really play themselves. I sang along with Doris Day's *How much is that doggy in the window?* or Max Bygraves singing *I'm a pink toothbrush.*

When Manfred was holding me tight, leaning out of the bedroom window, I believed I could do it, I knew I could fly. I had studied the birds carefully and half believed that if I flapped my arms up and down in a slow graceful movement, they would become wings. What he was nurturing was the belief that I could fly and of course I did fly through my imagination.

My mother showed me how I could become a fish. I wrapped my arms tightly round her neck and we sang *Waltzing Matilda* as she threw me from side to side in the water. She held my little body with my hands locked above my head. I floated, carried by the water, weightless. Through half-closed eyes I could see dancing diamonds around me. I pretended to be a mermaid whenever there was a stream, a lake, the sea and even the bathtub. I'd swim for hours.

When I was a teenager we often shared long swims at the seaside.

"Let's swim out," she'd say, ignoring my frantic father on the shore. "Don't look back, keep your eye on the horizon...... swim out."

She'd swim and tell me her old swimming stories. Although the water might be choppy she could breathe evenly, swim her steady sidestroke and talk at the same time. We'd settle down for a long side by side swim.

"We'd be the first to the Hallensee," she said. "I'd dive in."

"How could you dive on a lakeside?"

"Oh they had springboards."

"Where?"

"You'd swim out to a floating platform in the middle of the lake and there would be a springboard to dive from."

"Were you out of your depth?"

"I never thought about it."

She does now, always reminding me to be sure I can get back if I'm out of my depth.

"Was granny or your dad watching you?" I knew about worried parents standing on the edge holding a towel.

"No of course not, I went on my own; I was often the only girl who dared dive in."

Freedom, this sounded good, not like Cookridge Street Baths in the centre of Leeds, a building blackened with northern soot and freezing changing rooms.

"I'd wear my costume under my clothes then whip them off and be in the water as soon as we arrived. I'd swim out as fast as I could. I wanted to be first on the diving board."

"Was it cold?"

"Yes, yes it took your breath away at first but then you tingled all over and swam faster and faster."

"Did you crawl?"

"No, breaststroke was my best. I could swim long periods doing breaststroke. Crawl would have been better, that's why I've taught you crawl."

"Did you wear a cap?"

"Never."

I imagined red curls, dark with water, clinging to her head. Now, we both wore close-fitting rubber caps, with a narrow strap under the chin.

"Did you wear a bikini?"

"Don't be silly, I swam properly, I wasn't a pin-up girl. We wore knitted costumes in those days; I think Frieda made me one."

I was wearing my navy blue school costume as we swam, it was elasticated and I had sewn badges from different countries all over it. In their letters aunties had requested that our distant relatives send a small cloth badge for my swimming costume. I wore them proudly. I was bringing the family from across the water together in the water.

"We'd swim for a while and then sit around in a cafe, sharing cafe cognac one between eight of us."

"What did you talk about?"

"How to emigrate. What country would take us in."

"Did you ever talk about staying in touch?"

She is silent we're both doing breaststroke in perfect rhythm, still swimming out, I'm listening to the sound of my own breathing, worrying that we should turn around, I don't speak.

"Always keep in touch with your friends," she says. "I couldn't."

I turn around, my father is a tiny speck on the shore. I strike out swimming crawl back to him. She follows.

Adolescence

Contrast the Hallensee with Roundhay Girls High School annual swimming gala. Long forms from the gym were placed along the sides of our swimming pool. The whole school was gasping and sweating. The green caps were the non-swimmers, or just feet-off-the-bottom, they performed short displays. The cherry caps demonstrated lengths in various strokes. Then came white caps, there were tests to reach this level, including life-saving which I passed aged fourteen. I raced backstroke in the gala, smashed my way through the water and crashed into the side, unable to swim in a straight line. The school laughed and applauded, but I was embarrassed and red-faced. In my mind's eye I was an elegant mermaid, in reality a dumpy clown.

Assembly

The Jewish girls were excused from the daily general school assembly, so they would not be compelled to utter the words "Jesus Christ".

My father was adamant that I would do the opposite; he wrote a polite note to the head teacher on blue Basildon Bond paper in his best formal English. He begged to be excused for making a fuss, but was insisting that I was not withdrawn.

> *Esteemed Miss Lee*
> *It is with sincere apology for your time I write to request from you about my daughter in Assembly.... I wish her in all circumstances to attend. She must pray with everyone.*

I struggled with this paradox.

"But daddy.... other Jewish girls brought notes to school saying that they can't attend Christian prayers."

I belonged with the others, swinging on pegs in the cloakroom and whispering until we filed in silently for notices when the religious bit was over.

"No," he said, "everyone prays to the same God. If he's good enough for the English he's good enough for you."

I sighed, embarrassed. This meant more explanations, to the Jewish girls, to the rest of my class, to the teacher. I always seemed to be explaining something such as why my parents had a funny accent, why my sandwiches didn't have the same bread as theirs.

So I stood in the middle of all the little English girls singing *All Things Bright and Beautiful* at full volume. I closed my eyes and folded my hands in readiness for the Lord's Prayer, but sucked my pigtails doubtfully when we came to the bit where everyone said "THROUGH JESUS CHRIST OUR LORD, AMEN."

How many are six million? Sometimes I stood in assembly, the hall, packed with eight hundred girls. How much bigger would the school hall have to be? I look out of the window, how many people could be packed on to the street? Two thousand, three thousand? How many streets would you need for six million?

I was once in a jam-packed Wembley stadium. As the concert started I looked round. This is it, I thought. How many people does Wembley hold? One hundred and fifty thousand. That's all. The biggest stadium in the world, in Brazil, holds one hundred and seventy five thousand. Where would six million fit? How do you measure them? Six million Jews; I'm never happy in a crowd.

I was fifteen and longed to go dancing but was never allowed to go to the Mecca ballroom in Leeds. I finally went to a dance at the Astoria down the road. I went with friends but wasn't allowed lipstick or high heels and only three petticoats, so I carried lipstick and white kitten heels in a vinyl duffle bag, lemon checks. I wore my petticoats, stiffened with sugar water underneath a pink dress with a wide white plastic belt, with lacing down the front called a "waspie", puffed sleeves and a heart-shaped neckline. I tried to create a cleavage but hadn't heard of using chicken fillets and the blobs of cotton wool kept falling out of my miniscule bra. I was flat as a pancake, pushing the sides of my chest together hopefully to show an incline. The role models of that era were Marilyn Monroe, Sophia Loren, Gina Lollobrigida, the hour-glass look which I would eventually grow into just as Twiggy and the era of the stick insect emerged. I met my friends at the bus stop and we sat at the top of the bus squinting into tiny mirrors applying our Outdoor Girl two and sixpenny lipsticks in candy floss pink.

I walked stiffly in my suspender belt and nylons that tended to wrinkle slightly around my ankles. If I smoothed them out my finger made a hole or at least a ladder which would be mended with clear nail varnish. I wasn't allowed nail varnish, mascara, rouge or green eye shadow.

The long hall had a wooden floor smelling of wax polish. The band was playing an Acker Bilk number, a few old couples were drifting around the centre of the hall waltzing, the lights were low, there was a glitter ball. The boys lined up against one wall, Brylcreamed hair, forelocks falling over one eye, drainpipe trousers, long jackets with velvet collars, "bootlace" ties and "winklepicker" shoes. They were smoking. The girls were lined up against the other wall. It reminded me of battlefields during the Civil War, Oliver Cromwell and King Charles. How would we all advance to the middle I wondered, after the fight what would the debris be left there?

It wasn't fair; my mother had climbed out of grandmother's flat in Berlin to dance the night away in some dimly lit café fuelled by brandy, dancing the tango, pursued by delectable young European men. It sounded sophisticated, tantalising, risqué certainly not what was before me in the Astoria Ballroom, Harehills, Leeds where my own pursuit of delicious decadence began. I knew it was hopeless, the girls eventually formed a circle cutting out the tedious, posturing boys altogether. We danced round our handbags in a circle, mincing, posing, fluttering our eyelashes, exuding the smell of cheap perfume and hair lacquer in our beehive hair. We wiggled our teenage bums and swayed our non-existent hips to each other in the safety of that circle, knowing that we were formidable untouchables to those silly smoking boys. We wanted something different but didn't know what.

My brother would arrive at the door to fetch me, that wasn't fair either. The other girls were allowed to go home by bus. Maybe I was missing a secret assignation on the bus, a moment of passion on the top deck without the dividing dance floor. My brother would wait in his van outside in the cold, a cigarette hanging out of his mouth, absorbed in a James Dean impersonation. He'd rev the engine and speed up Roundhay Road pretending he was in a sports car. We would be laughing and joking in seconds and I would be safely dropped home while he whizzed towards the lights of Leeds in pursuit of his own adventures.

Once in my bedroom I didn't mind really. I twiddled the knobs of the maroon radio to find radio Luxembourg and daydreamed, gazing into darkness listening to Buddy Holly, wishing I was grown up and wearing stilettos and blood red lipstick.

I am seventeen and sit in Mark Green's room in Bodington Hall. We kiss for hours; I'm hot and it's getting boring but I don't want to signal my willingness to get to the next stage which involves removing my jumper. I look over his shoulder at the red flag pinned on the wall, the hammer and sickle. I am puzzling its meaning and listening to Miriam Makeba.

I was good at some subjects, I was bad at others. There was little in between. I coasted through school in the D stream, often behaving badly, sometimes working desperately hard. I changed my attitude daily like my hairstyle or my handwriting.

Writing was difficult and biros were not allowed. I often smeared the brown diluted ink across the page as I wrote with a pen dipped into the inkwells at the corner of the wooden desk. I was given a fountain pen once, but that soon was lost or traded for a coloured hair ribbon.

We read a different Shakespeare play every year. I was fourteen when *The Merchant of Venice* was chosen as the school play. Rehearsals were at four o'clock right through the winter term. We brought our tea and some girls brought a flask with Horlicks. We swapped cakes and biscuits. The smell of potted meat sandwiches wafted from the back of the hall. I attended every rehearsal even when they weren't my scenes. I watched Miss King coax the characters out of the schoolgirls standing on the stage in their navy tunics, cardigans with a white stripe and coloured house badges on their lapels.

I whispered the words of the text with them, often puzzling over the meaning of the words. At first it seemed indecipherable, then slowly the meaning would filter through, just by studying the words and connecting them to present day English. I was used to this process. I listened to German conversation at home and picked out recognisable words and deduced the meaning from the context. Being brought up by foreigners was very useful during our school Shakespeare rehearsals. Later, hurrying home in the dark, the words turned in my brain.

I felt uncomfortable that no-one mentioned Shylock was Jewish. No one discussed the play's anti-semitic stereotyping. The girl playing Shylock was experimenting with foreign accents. I watched silently. She said she had never met anyone foreign, never heard anyone speak English with a foreign accent. She had no TV. The only accents were German baddies in post-war films. Germans were the baddies, Shylock the Jew seemed a baddie. I never mentioned this to my family. I discouraged my parents from coming to see the play. They never need know about Shylock, the Jew. It was a pity because I had fencing lessons for the fight scenes and I would have been proud for them to see me fence on stage.

In the sixth form at school we were allowed to drink coffee indoors at break. We still wore uniform, no longer a gymslip but a navy pleated skirt which we rolled up at the waist to reach well above the knees. The rule was no more than three petticoats. We wore a special sixth form tie. I was now supposed to wash my white blouses myself every day, but kept forgetting. I wore them for the second day with a curled collar and grimy cuffs. Eventually my prefect's badge was removed because I was setting a bad example to younger girls by not keeping my uniform pristine. I wore my beret at a jaunty angle, the badge folded under round the back and a pair of sunglasses in my pocket ready to wear as I came out of the school gates.

In 1963, two poems I had written were broadcast on *The Northern Drift*, a radio programme consisting of sketches, songs and poetry about the north of England. It was produced by Alfred Bradley in the old Leeds Studio1 on Woodhouse Lane and broadcast on the Third Programme. He invited me in to the studio where I sat, listening to the performers northern accents, still a rarity on the BBC. Later I listened to the group of socialist performers and writers in Whitelock's Ale House, Leeds. These included novelists Stan Barstow, Alan Sillitoe, David Storey, Henry Livings, playwright Shelagh Delaney and the marvellous Geordie folk singer, Alex Glasgow. They were developing sharp socialist songs and pieces of dialogue. These would become scripts, read out in the pub, performed on the radio and later adapted for the Theatre in the Round, in Scarborough. They discussed Labour politics, definitively old labour, presenting a polarised view of society as represented in the Yorkshire mill towns: the bosses and the workers. They displayed a revolutionary fervour that had emerged from the backstreet slums of their own or their kitchen-sink heroes' childhoods. My own immigrant granddad had been a mill owner, one of the bosses, aspiring to the English bourgeoisie. Here I was, finding my place, with a group of writers who were the voice of the working class; presenting a way of life that was as foreign to me as a bottle of brown sauce on a plastic tablecloth.

> *O, My Daddy is a left-wing intellectual*
> *But he really thought the Beatles were a gas*
> *Mind, he didn't like their music*
> *or their haircuts and the rest*
> *He liked them 'cause they were from the working class.*
> Alex Glasgow

She stands in the silence of the night, frost biting her fingers and toes, the breath from her mouth turning white.

There is a rustling from the corners of the square; silhouettes emerge from inky darkness and the church bells chime 4 am.

She gasps as hundreds of lanterns light up ghostly sheep's' heads, long beaked pelicans, a huge pig's snout and   toothless smiles brushing side by side.

The shrill sound of the flutes resonates over the beating of the drums. She twists and turns caught up in an endless stream of scaley fish heads, grotesque Punchinellos, bobbing lights and the Angel of Death.

Zero, a girl who has emerged from the egg with beating wings has a bird's head.

PART FOUR

Imagine Belonging

Community is nowadays another name for paradise lost - but one to which we dearly hope to return, and so we feverishly seek the roads that may bring us there.....
Zygmunt Bauman
Community: Seeking Safety in an Insecure World: 2001

Chapter 9

We were the first generation of girls to take our education for granted and assume it was our right to reach university. I also took my equality for granted, seeing the opportunities, denied to my mother and grandmother, which were now within my grasp. It was the decade that began with Germaine Greer and ended with Margaret Thatcher.

Domesticity had continued to be paramount in the definition of women's role in society during the fifties. Women could only obtain a mortgage if a man countersigned her documents. We young women were crossing the bridge of education, but still presenting ourselves as prim and respectable. Marriage continued to be the ultimate goal, but we were encouraged to dream. If we worked hard we could have everything, scholarships to university, money and even a Prince Charming!

For my university interview in 1963 I wore a jersey suit with a pencil skirt below the knee, suspenders for my nylon stockings and short white nylon gloves. My hair was in a French pleat. An Audrey Hepburn scarf was knotted at my throat and flyaway sunglasses. I studied Drama, a new degree course, at Manchester University.

I participated in a student production of *The Sport of My Mad Mother* by Ann Jellicoe, a play written in the rhythms and cadences of teenage youngsters on a housing estate. Here were my first steps away from a formal script and on to the vernacular of the street. I was taught by Stephen Joseph, whose mission had been to democratise theatre and make it more accessible, transcending the class system. His inspirational energy shaped my lasting disregard for the establishment. His own eclectic talent encouraged me to explore a range of skills and knowledge, not to specialise or become an expert in one area. Stephen's dreams of a theatre which would be relevant to all walks of life was the spark that eventually lit the tinder box of my running through the streets of Leeds, London, Ashkelon and Melbourne with a loudhailer followed by processions of local children.

I was still a teenager when I encountered his lone voice challenging the establishment. His revolutionary charisma and leadership would resonate as my own working life spanned theatre, inner city neighbourhoods and National Health Service. He died in 1967 and I lost my first teacher. I had been initiated into a stance against the status quo. The counter-culture was a tornado sweeping towards our shores. I was ready for it.

I was yet to discover the socialist music, folk songs of Ewan McColl, his collaboration with Charles Parker and the radio ballads. These used the words of fishermen, travellers, teenagers, sometimes as monologue, sometimes as words of a song, a mix of words and music.

For my graduation in 1966 I wore a black leather jacket, black mini skirt fishnet tights and bright red suede high heels. My hair was short, a dark mop like the Beatles, a Gauloises cigarette hanging from the corner of my mouth and heavy black eyeliner. The fifties were defined by our parents still reeling from cataclysmic shifts the war and its aftermath had made on their lives. We lay watching them as they pushed our prams deeper into suburbia and we noticed how they were becoming fossilized resisting any idea of change. We would redefine ourselves and the world we inhabited. We wanted new hope, determined to become who we wanted to be. My mum was right, we girls would seize the day.

Manchester 1967

I assisted on a community play at the Manchester Library Theatre, *The Rising Generation* by Anne Jellico, directed by Philip

Hedley. This play was written for a cast of a hundred children participating through improvisation. They drew on their observations of teachers, parents, characters in their everyday lives, they copied a gait, an accent, a snippet of dialogue.

This was my introduction to improvisation, mining our own perceptions and experiences, and turning them into a drama. It came from within our own knowledge and skill. It did not demand studying or learning a script, but required interdependence, collaboration and close listening instead.

Children watched old ladies cross the road, toddlers taking their first steps, dads holding a pint. They logged the movements, the atmosphere and the emotion, then reproduced it, slowly adding dialogue, forming relationships between invented characters, eventually edging towards a script.

Closely related were the documentary plays (more recently re-defined as verbatim theatre) developed by Peter Cheeseman, in his community based repertory theatre. Local events, stories and the concerns that impacted ordinary lives were recounted to actors. Themes included the miners' strike, the campaign to save the steel works, the history of the Potteries. Peter's company developed these stories into plays, using the original words and music on stage. He kept editorial control of the material but used original recordings in performances.

"You find someone with a story, Carry, record them and keep it safe, it's a treasure, one day it will be listened to."

I was very influenced by Peter's commitment to authentic representation of material. My quest would be to find ways of giving editorial control to the original narrators. I now wanted to create dramas about real people, performed where they would resonate. This meant coming out of the theatre and into the streets or community centres, dog-training hall or shopping precinct. Any natural gathering place could become a performance area. Ten years later these ideas would crystallise in *Sweet Sixteen*.

***

We had something to say, not something to sell
SuzeRotolo
A memoir of Greenwich Village in the sixties

I'm running away from the fifties, out of the shadows of Berlin that were cast across my parent's lives, my granny's neat clothes, my Aunty Frieda's cotton overall, Saturday afternoons and the music of Brahms and Schubert on the BBC radio Third Programme, evoking the world they had lost. It has become a world I no longer wish to inhabit. So here I am, breaking free from the buttoned-up German high art, speeding towards the avant-garde, yet not knowing what I wanted to challenge. I find my peer group, also searching for unpredictability and risk. We're all looking for a way of life, more than just a way of working; we question behaviour both within relationships, and within society. Our wish is to create contexts based on shared human values and beliefs. Those of us who eagerly became part of the counterculture were influenced by Marxism, communism, socialism, anarchism (and all their overlaps). Across the individual rhetoric groups were unified by opposition to war, especially war in defence of capitalist expansion. The common cry was that the world needed to be changed.

We see ourselves as activists, our work at the grass roots is based on dreams of equality of opportunity and education. We experiment with the use of arts and media, hoping to give disadvantaged people a voice. We are committed to unleashing creativity in many forms, believing it to be the essence of all human life and that the potential to heal is embedded in the arts. The question for us is not simply where to work but for whom, and with whom. We belong on the street, in derelict buildings and squats. These are our homes and our theatres. We are collaborators, developing projects, writing scripts, rehearsing shows, sewing costumes, printing photographs.

We have little interest in money. State funding is available to experiment with social and artistic interventions for the most challenging people. We forge new ways of working. The roots of our work are not in tried and tested evidence-based practice but in innovation, respect, equality, action research and, above all, being ourselves. We take the arts out into the community, linking lives. John Lennon had proclaimed in 1968: I am a revolutionary artist. We became bricoloeurs, early re-cyclers, using waste to create art on the streets. Art and creativity was a right that belonged to everyone, not just an expression of the elite. I became part of the counter-culture.

Meanwhile the women's movement was gathering momentum. Harold Wilson's government and large agenda on massive public spending had led to an economic downturn. This was exacerbated by the death throes of key industries and subsequent unemployment. These issues were symbolised by derelict sites and massive urban decay led to crises within those communities.

My own generalist skills fit with the ethos of the time where experts and specialists are mistrusted, our aim is to transfer our knowledge and create social equality. My drama training makes me a natural collaborator and I fit comfortably within a movement of art in a social context.

My relentless energy propelled me through the next ten years; a punishing schedule week after week with different groups, street theatre in both London and Leeds, then in Milton Keynes before travelling abroad, devising street shows and projects about immigrants. This time has stayed forever in my bloodstream, it still spills out of my work and on to the pages of my writing.

At best our collective impassioned work sparked friendships based on trust, relationships formed through intense activity relying on wit, creativity and invention. We formed bonds lasting our lifetime. We were part of something, more than ourselves.

Being swept along by the tide of collectivism was sometimes exhausting. Occasionally I longed for solitude and found in the maelstrom of interdependence little opportunity to assess and develop the skills I was developing as an individual. My parents, aware of this, were sharply critical of my belligerent anti-career stance.

1968, my first move to London, sleeping on Aunty Martha's sofa. She is now over eighty, I am twenty-three.

She rents a top floor flat, with a kitchen on the landing, in Canfield Gardens, off the Finchley Road, refugee land. Black and white checked lino on the floor, frayed kilims and post-war G plan furniture left by the previous tenant. Sometimes I climb up to the top floor carrying her groceries and cook her spaghetti whilst she attends her French class. We eat at her round table covered with a green oilcloth.

Other times we stroll to Dudu, a local dress shop, press our noses against the window. We discuss the patterns, the shapes, the colours, the styles of the clothes on display. She sits watching me try on different garments and insists on choosing one, Laura Ashley with sprigged flowers. She fumbles for her purse, spilling ten-shilling notes over the counter whilst peering at a half-crown piece. I look round uneasily; she could have easily been pushed aside and her purse grabbed.

She buys me dinner at Dorice's, the restaurant frequented by ageing émigrés. We eat matjes herrings, sip Russian tea, and show our purchases to her friends; we sit chatting in German, until nightfall.

Whilst she snores quietly in her bedroom, I lie secretly entwined with an unwashed vegan in a skimpy jumper and odd socks who strums his guitar on the Berlin sofa until dawn, when we creep out to watch the sunrise over Primrose Hill.

She's in hospital. I arrive at the Royal Free, clutching flowers and a box of herrings. Where was she? The nurse points to a trolley being wheeled out of the doors opposite. "That's her," she says, "she just died a few minutes ago."

I sit on a bench in the corridor, eating the herrings with my fingers, oil dribbling down my chin.

Chapter 10

Underneath the Motorway, Notting Hill

I'm standing outside the Roundhouse in Camden, north London, distributing leaflets advertising an avant-garde theatre troupe from New York. My minuscule kaftan has an African print, butterflies embroidered around the hem. I'm wearing a silver ankle bracelet with tiny bells. My feet are bare: green nail varnish on grubby toes, fingers festooned with silver rings. My bra and the horrid flesh-coloured rubbery roll-on with suspenders have been discarded, never again nylon stockings. I am a free spirit in swinging London working as a part-time supply teacher. I use Beatles lyrics to inspire children's poetry writing.

> *Look for the girl with the sun in her eyes*
> *And she's gone*

This is when I meet a bearded American[1] with wild black hair, wearing a full-length rabbit fur coat. ED Berman invites me to sit underneath the Westway in Notting Hill improvising games with small children. I'm a willing player, clapping hands in a little circle under the motorway. We shout in order to be heard over the roar of the traffic above our heads. We all change places, we jump up and down, we mirror each other's movements, we pull funny faces and make up rhymes.

That damp November evening the children's smiling faces and exuberant participation enchanted me forever. I was

1 - The American, ED Berman, as a Harvard student had had been developing the theory and practice of children's games as a group process since 1957. It would later become known as Inter-Action Creative Game Method

destined to return many times to play these games: in a shop-front on Chalk Farm Road, clearing dog turds from the floor before sitting around in a circle and clapping hands, 'two claps, two spaces and in the spaces tell us...'

Leeds 1969

"What is it I need to understand about the education system and how children learn?" I asked.

I knew I wanted to work with children.

I had also reluctantly promised my parents I would teach for a year. I would then be awarded my teacher's number. My parents were adamant.

"You have to be able to earn your living, you need a qualification, and you never know when you might have to move."

I rent a flat off Chapeltown Road, furnished with orange boxes for kitchen units and paint the walls bright green. No three piece suites of the fifties. Nothing must match, everything is found through rummaging in a junk shop, lifted off a skip, plank and brick bookshelves, Indian bedspreads on the floor and on the wall, torn pieces of tissue paper glued to the windows instead of curtains. Always the sickly smell of patchouli josh sticks, mingling with the cannabis residue, stale cigarettes and empty wine bottles, a red scarf draped round a naked light bulb.

I am employed as a drama teacher in a girls' secondary school, Armley, Leeds. My classroom is transformed into a total arts environment. We write poems whilst marking the register, there are constantly changing exhibitions on the walls; I initiate drama clubs after school. At lunchtime, we rummage through dustbins making sculptures in the playground out of discarded materials.

The French teacher, reads extracts from Sartre to her pupils. The special needs teacher, Sandra, with rows of coloured beads around her neck, has a drooling yellow Labrador that snoozes underneath her desk; he occasionally emerges to lick the leg of a distressed pupil. He poses as a model for the daily life-drawing class. Sandra's classroom, as bright as her necklaces, is filled with plants, papier-maché puppets drying on the window ledge and textured fabric collages on the wall. I'm now a Leeds schoolteacher. I am learning how to hold a class's attention, show children how literature can shine a light on their own lives, invite them to tell stories of their own experiences. I stand in the rain on playground duty. I mark essays every evening and sit in my classroom until five o'clock helping little girls learn how to spell. I am relieved to be in an all-female environment and enjoy girls flourishing without distraction.

However, the London scene is always beckoning.

Because this appears to be a settled time, I find it unsettling. I can't allow myself to sail into calm waters. I still long to become part of the Bohemian life in London; Camden Town could be my new Weimar Republic, sex and decadence, the Berlin of my dreams, risen from the ashes.

I can't decide where to belong.

So I try to be in both places at once - the week in Leeds, the weekend in London.

London 1969-70

Friday night, school's out and I'm heading for London. I drive my Morris 10, bought for £8. It has large pink flowers with yellow borders on each door; a psychedelic car designed by the children in my class. I set off down the M1, liver sausage sandwiches for my tea, singing Me and Bobby McGee all the way, freedom of the road, my Jack Kerouac moments.

I'm happiest in my little car between one world and the other; the journey down the M1 is a no-man's land.

I turn into Prince of Wales Road. The aroma of cannabis drifts through the car window. The back streets of Camden are lined with squats. Fabrics purchased in the souks of Morocco, bright colours faded by the sun are pinned with drawing pins across the windows, opaque with dirt. The smell of sour milk from unwashed milk bottles, women with kerchiefs on their heads and many rows of beads, men with shoulder length hair and beards of varying lengths from bushy to straggly, grey babies in rickety buggies.

I arrive, hungry after the three-hour journey and find the Inter-Action[2] office humming with activity although it is 10'clock at night. I lick a hundred envelopes, the mailshot for a new show. Everyone works together to catch the midnight post at Mount Pleasant post office.

I'm even hungrier.

We eventually eat after 11pm at the Greek restaurant in Camden Town, with olive trees outside the front door. We share steaming Kleftikos, keep awake with a couple of Turkish Delights and black, syrupy coffee served in tiny cups.

Later we climb the stairs to a top floor Covent Garden flat, a dimly lit room, someone strumming a guitar, drinking schnapps, smoking a joint. My teaching day up in Yorkshire was a million miles away,

Saturday night, we rush to Marine Ices on Chalk Farm Road and buy large metal tubs of ice cream before cramming into the dark wood panelled office. Tonight the founders of Scotland Road Free School, Liverpool, are presenting their work. I plop a lump of chocolate ice cream into my mug of coffee and sit cross-legged on the floor. I am transported into the description of the school which allows children to choose what they learn, invites local community groups to support their learning, and uses the arts as the route to literacy, numeracy and social skills. They also describe their fight for funding. I see the local council as an enemy, only choosing to uphold the status quo. I see us all united in the fight for the continued right to experiment.

Sunday and the chimes of midnight, I grab a couple of cans of coke, a packet of crisps, jump into my flower car and head north planning my lessons for Monday as I drive.

Inter-Action became a provocative social action and community arts organisation, which breathed new life into the

---

2 - Inter-Action was a living and working community, housed in short life property leased from Camden Council. Everyone worked long hours, was paid equally, and took turns to shop and cook for sixty people. Inter-Action challenged mainstream theatre by creating a venue for experimental writing and performance in the heart of London's West End. Established writers contributed to the first season of gay plays in Britain, the first season of plays by women, the first season addressing Black issues. Inter-Action also created highly visible events on the street. In 1978, before the local elections, a piano without black keys was delivered to the home of the National Front candidate.

derelict sites and sink estates, Britain's inner city landscape of the 70s. Feral arts and wild ideas created new communities.

There was little time in Inter-Action to ruminate on ideas. A new project was suggested, a proposal written, endorsements from relevant experts gathered, an appropriate source for funding targeted, the project field-tested, launched and often replicated by groups around the country within a few months. The national movement of City Farms emerged in this way.

ED Berman[3] became my second teacher. He challenged the establishment and influenced social and artistic thinking further than Stephen Joseph managed before his time ran out. They both shared immediacy, pragmatism and inspirational leadership.

A door is pushed open.

I am poised on the threshold of an urban kibbutz, collective living and working together.

I knit through meetings, committees of three and votes for programmes, votes for washing up coffee cups.

I am given hand-printed books about the barefoot doctor, making leather sandals.

Voices call out, inviting me to sign up for the washing up rotas, telling me it's my turn to cook dinner: "Remember the must-have-meats…and don't forget the cauliflower cheese for the vegetarians."

"And don't forget it's your turn on the toilet cleaning rota."

Come into our urban jungle in the heart of London, they all entice me…

The underground roars through the station.

Welcome to the metropolis.

Turn your whites pink as you throw them into our washes of mixed coloureds, spinning round in circles 24 hours per day.

3 - Ed Berman, founder of Inter-Action,(1968) was a major influence on theatre, social and community arts initiatives from the late sixties. He was, an immigrant and an outsider, implementing projects of social innovation.. ED currently promotes "Rational activism" , a positive type of activism which leads to popular good will and in certain cases, increased profits. He still runs Inter-Action with the help of a number of interns and volunteers. In 2014 he was elected the Chair of the newly formed Rhodes Scholars in Britain charity.

Join the circus, join the band,
Why don't you come with us?
Everyone is welcome.
You can have lots of fun with us.

Colonel Crackpot' Christmas Circus - 1971

Make a Newspaper - 1980

Chapter 11

Leeds 1970

The flower car trundles up and down the M1, weekly between Chapeltown, Leeds, and Camden Town, London, for maybe a year, maybe two or three. When it finally grinds to a halt its replaced by a battered green mini, a car with its own radio, heaven!

I wanted to be in the education system at the same time as being against it. I positioned myself inside society, at the same time as being against society. I nurtured a fantasy of creating a new order.

I leave teaching and move in with a collective of artists in Leeds, never thinking of job security, a steady income, a home. Who needs new clothes? There are Oxfam shops. Property is theft! We pool our possessions. Gone are my record player, vinyl collection and camera. I grab an electric blanket and a copy of the Whole Earth catalogue instead. I reinforce my patterns of staying on the edge. I have one foot in Inter-Action and one foot in Leeds.

I work two days a week at the Jacob Kramer branch College of Art School for Vocational Students. I am part of the Liberal Arts department. Students were required to work on projects that combined their disciplines. They are foundation fine art, fashion, graphics and photography students. My projects include a blue week (wearing and making blue clothes, dying hair blue creating a totally blue environment, writing blue poetry, singing the blues, eating blue mashed potato). Another project is building a soft and sensory tunnel in a school for children with disabilities.

We build shelters out on the Yorkshire Moors, sleep in them under a cold, white moon and record sounds of the night to accompany images, used later in a multimedia installation. We build giants out of waste and found materials and create a final happening at night. One giant is constructed out of wire wrapped in rags. These are soaked in petrol and set alight, flaming giants light up the night sky.

The Leeds education authority awards me a grant to lead improvisation workshops with young people on Saturdays. My collaborators are sociology graduates, drama and art students. We workshop an improvised play, which is eventually scripted by Brian Thompson. The theme is a protest *Give us an Idea to Stop the Traffic*. It involves large numbers of adolescents clad in cheesecloth carrying banners through the audience and chanting anti-capitalist slogans. It is performed at Swarthmore Further Education Centre and Leeds Art Gallery.

Another performance was the 'Bread Show', little vignettes about the evil of money. The climax was throwing chocolate gold coins at the audience.

The workshop developed street theatre, our procession travelled to Quarry Hill Flats Leeds. I gathered children using a loudhailer. We played games and sang rhyming songs on the street corners. Our play presented a conflict to be resolved by the audience. We performed every Sunday morning in a different area of the city.

I felt slightly daunted by the empty streets but we always gathered a group of small children with our guitar and a few games. We visited the chosen site a few days prior to the performance, working out where it was safe to perform, where we wouldn't wake anyone up and where we could create a circle without treading on dog poo or broken glass.

Sunday mornings on the streets of Leeds, November afternoons under London's Westway, my apprenticeship in community arts.

Interplay 1972

Armley, Leeds, was a solid working-class community, many still living in 19th century back-to-back houses, with outside 'lavvies' and cobbled streets. There was considerable derelict land but very limited access to parks or open space.

We are a group of artists and activists, humanists, socialists, liberals, Quakers, sociology graduates. We are united by a belief in social and political empowerment through the arts; supported by Inter-Action we form Interplay in 1972, registering it as a charity. We are committed enough to subsist on poverty wages and some members lived in a shared house. We eat together and pay ourselves £7 per week. We are always seen as outsiders, or 'students', by the local community.

The development of theatre in challenging contexts and with vulnerable participants becomes the focus of our work. We receive a small grant from the Yorkshire Arts Association and the Leeds Education Department. We work in the shadow of a large Victorian jail where the last public hanging had taken place in 1864.

Radical arts groups around the country were receiving council funding to deliver summer holiday programmes. National and local organisations highlight the importance of play, adventure playgrounds emerge, soft rooms for babies and toddlers, play buses.

The leaders of these groups were usually men. I often found myself in a world full of young, bearded men, accustomed to taking the spotlight. They were assured in their roles, eager to challenge the mainstream with loud voices and confident rhetoric. The women were there, at the heart of the work and still sitting in the office, in administrative roles, behind the men with power.

As a sixth former I had entered a left-wing world of northern writers and directors. It was a world comprised mainly of men, eager to write about class equality, sing about poverty, but I hardly heard any conversation about the role of women, rarely a woman's voice in those sessions in the pub. I had an impression of Her Indoors, the wife, removed from this world of ideas and collaboration. I was never at ease, wrong class, wrong gender.

Art

> *Seeing comes before words. The child looks and*
> *recognizes before it can speak.*
> John Berger - 1972

We are standing on a play site in the sunshine, surrounded by children. Each one holds a plastic bag twisted into different shape into which they had poured plaster of Paris, the consistency of thick cream. Now they held the bags aloft, feeling the chemical change between their hands as the plaster slowly became hard. We wait for it to harden, then peel away the plastic and marvel at the twists and hollows of the creamy white sculpture in our hands. We have created a lunar landscape of rocks and stalagmites.

Artist Liz Leyh[4] shows me the shapes and colours of the cobbles under my feet. I notice the roofscapes above my head. She shows me that things can look like other things; the Eiffel Tower can look like a bone, the cloud can look like a dragon breathing fire, and the dog's tail is a sweeping brush.

I sit drawing in her studio:

"Carry if you practice drawing ten minutes every day, you'll be able to draw, and it's another language. It's no different to learning French; today it's the past tense. This week you're going to draw the plant for ten minutes every couple of hours throughout the day, just watching where the shadow changes."

Liz sends me a parcel of a hundred lovely things: bits of shiny ribbon, a piece of lace and beads, feathers from a pillowcase to be dyed with coloured inks, crystals shards of glass to represent the stars or an eye for the stork, cellophane sweet wrappers which we wash so they can be used as lighting gel for a shadow play. When my head is too full of words she

---

4 - Liz Leyh received the first bursary grant awarded by the Arts Council of Great Britain for a New Town artist's residency. She became town artist in Milton Keynes in the mid-seventies. She worked with residents to design and make sculptures and other art works in public places. The famous "Concrete Cows" are a reminder of her residency.
When working in Inter-Action Liz wrote and illustrated the book Concrete Sculpture published by Inter-Action. She also wrote Children Make Sculpture, published, by Van Nostrand Reinhold, 1974

sends a tortoise on a card, on a chain, or two perfectly carved peas nestling in a tiny pod she has just completed, her hands always busy while waiting for the bus.

I create order for a day on a play site. I lay out all the tools, sharpening the coloured pencils and lining them up in gradients of colour. I slice off the grubby edges of the white eraser. I take chalks out of new packets and decant them into small freezer bags to make them last. I arrange materials in cardboard shoeboxes, begged from local shops (each volunteer play leader collects them in the morning before going on site).

We perform in natural meeting places. Design was adapted to the street environment in banners, posters, giant masks and loudhailers. We are realising Stephen Joseph's dream by moving out of the elitist concert hall, theatre or art gallery onto the street, the school, the community centre, the pub, moving closer to everyday life in the inner city. Our pop-up performances land on the streets and derelict play sites, in pubs and homes. The heart of our endeavour is the creating and building of community.

Stephen Joseph had abandoned the proscenium arch stage and built his theatre-in-the-round with an audience on all sides; we are now performing around our audience from corner-to-corner. We work together and build on each other's ideas. We create participatory techniques, connecting people of all ages together. We have rejected formal scripts repeating performance after performance. We move in and out of improvisation alongside our audiences.

Ask your Mum if you can come, we chanted, *to Strawberry Lane, right now.* We wave banners with the information painted in bright colours. We stop on corners, sing a song, play a game, invite children to participate and tell jokes, to make up their own verses to the song, demonstrate their dance. Our raggle-taggle, joyous processions of games and music made us all, at those moments, celebrities of the street.

Keep the Circle Moving - Games, London 1970-72

*How we play the game may turn out to be more
important than we imagine, for it signifies nothing
less than our way of being in the world*
George Leonard 1972

I am sitting cross-legged in a circle of children. There is a little
girl in scarlet on the edge, anxiously sucking the edge of her
tee-shirt. I make a space next to me and beckon to her, she
reaches for my outstretched hand and I draw her in.

Clap, clap, space, space - let's try it altogether. The clapping
erupts around the circle. Most of the children understand first
time and are guided by me, counting the claps and then the spaces.
We practice. The circle has no end and no beginning, we are all
equal, and we all belong there doing the same simple action.

Next, in the spaces say "hello". This travels round the
circle, once we start everyone is the same, little voices say
"hello" - whispering, shouting, squeaking, one or two squirm a
little in their chairs, too shy to say the word, little girl in scarlet
has her head down.

I'm always looking out for the ones who don't fit - the
outsiders. I patiently work the circle again, more join in. I find
the simplest action in the spaces, just the lightest touch on a
neighbour's sleeve. The movement travels round the circle, like
an electric impulse, when it arrives back with me I feel the
lightest touch, I look down at the little girl in scarlet, we smile.

The actions of stepping in and staying out, taking turns,
holding the circle together, even sabotaging, create a sense of
community and belonging. Children use actions alongside
their words instinctively to enhance their ideas.

I was learning to engage and hold the attention of chaotic
children by combining and recombining sequences of games.
They played in pairs, sometimes in larger groups, sometimes
one person in the centre of as circle. Every games session
created its mini-community for that moment in time, taking
turns, watching, contributing. No one is top of the class at
playing games, everyone can join in some of the time, without
speaking English, in a wheelchair, with hearing loss.

Games representing democratic participation were fashionable in the 1960s and 1970s. Many books of games were written in the UK and in the US. Across the Atlantic, giant canopies of parachute silk fluttered over delighted children in classrooms and sports fields.

The boy is kneeling before a roll of newsprint holding a brush. He dips it into red paint and draws a squiggly line. A girl carefully lifts another brush dipped into emerald and makes new marks criss-crossing down the paper. When everyone has had a turn the children sit back on their heels and admire their work.

"It's a map, look those are roads we can walk along."

"Yes and the green dots are trees in summer."

"Those blobs are scary footprints in the mud"

"It's been raining"

"I can see purple hills far away"

"What's on the other side?" "Miss let's paint the other side of the purple hills."

We do, this time painting with words, adding a little to the story as it passes from one to the other. The game has taken us to a land over the hills and far away, a land of dreams and hope, travelling through darkness and despair, metaphors of the imagination. By the time they have played several games of words and completed many paintings they have populated their land with flora and fauna, food for the weird and wonderful creatures, which are going to reside on a relief concrete mural and form play structures interspersed with trees on their playground of many colours.

Theatre Leeds 1972

I am leading a street procession as Merlin, the wizard. I wear a wig of silver-sprayed wool, a dark blue robe down to my feet, embellished with silver stars and golden moons. I carry a staff in one hand and a loudhailer in the other; sweat drips down my nose. We have decorated the streets the previous night. Banners are strung across the narrow alleys inviting everyone to join King Arthur on Strawberry Lane, the bombsite designated to become Camelot.

The procession is heralded at dawn by a huge dragon walking the streets billowing smoke, tended by his keeper. A derelict house is turned into the façade of a castle, with a damsel in distress trapped at the top. During the procession, hundreds of children practise rescuing her and she triumphantly joins the procession. Arthur pulls the sword out of the stone and I crown him with his foil crown. We invite all the children to join us for the following three weeks to become Knights of the Round Table. This becomes the seat of democracy in Armley, performances at the end of each day and long discussions, resolved by voting on issues ranging from hitting and bullying, to dancing and performing.

I have a hospital appointment for a termination that afternoon so I can't start building Camelot. I am pretending I don't care. I couldn't even tell my lover when I found I was pregnant. "Nothing to do with me," he would have said, "I never promised you anything."

The era of the pill was just beginning. There had been many times when I had crouched in the dark, freezing cold, in an outside toilet to insert my contraceptive cap. I had waited for the pill, but by the time I could use it the idea of sexual freedom and no commitment had become less enticing.

I speak to my Leeds GP who insists I tell my parents. I'm twenty-seven, an adult, making my own choices. Besides I was hardly in contact with my parents; their bewilderment at my career choice had led to many rows and hostility. I slam the door of his surgery, furious, and drive the Flower car to Marie Stopes in London. It's 1972. Women were now entitled by law to an abortion. I will exercise my rights to my own personal sexual freedom.

We are the generation of women who juggle work with domesticity. Our daughters will become the women who would have it all, career and young children. They would struggle with impossible choices. I was learning that magic would not come from Merlin the wizard of the streets.

I'm back on site, hammering Camelot into existence. In the centre of our castle, made out of railway sleepers and old doors, is a large wooden circle, symbolic of the round table. Everyone at the end of the day sits round and watches performances. Everyone has an equal say, is allowed to speak when holding the conch. The youngest child has a vote and every voice is heard, no matter how small.

At night we gather in an old community building, loaned to us for the summer period, to eat and to analyse the day's events. We discuss individual children, the difficulties they present. There are debates on how to support children who show us their anger, throw bricks at us during round table meetings, how to support withdrawn children longing to participate, how to diffuse confrontation. There are arguments about smacking; one volunteer is voted out of the project because he has smacked a child on the play site. We celebrate moments of joy and the feeling of community onsite. We argue about storing the materials, how to organise the next day's activities. Everything is decided by vote, everyone takes their turn with each job, the cleaning of the toilets, cooking the communal meal, talking to the funders and leading activities on the site. Discussions continue long after the meal and by 10.30pm we are still organising our materials for the next day and writing up our notes.

During the final week, parents collect money for the barbecue and bonfire, the grand celebration and finale of the whole programme. Camelot would be burnt.

Children and parents come out at night in a procession carrying flares, playing music and dancing together. They fasten fireworks to the wooden structures built during the summer. Families toast marshmallows over the barbecue, grill sausages and bake potatoes wrapped in tin foil.

We had started with a procession and ended with a barbecue.

Children gaze in awe at the huge flames as Camelot burns and late into the night we still sit around the embers, our faces across the circle glowing in the light of the flames.

A student volunteer wearing flared trousers and a bandana plays the guitar, accompanying us as we sing *We shall overcome* and *Blowin' in the wind*.

When I was small, we played grandmother's footsteps; the leader turned their back and we crept up slowly behind; always weighing up whether the leader would turn round. The winner was the first person to touch the leader's shoulder while we were creeping up. I could never creep, I always made a dash for it, I could never cover ground slowly and carefully.

In the same way I swirled through the seventies, feet always moving to create a new group. It was a time of action and intervention.

Chapter 12

Womens' Movement, London 1972

The second wave of feminism had broken on the shores of America and was taking hold here, through the conferences of the early seventies, the reclaim-the-night marches on the streets, writing in periodicals and books.

While our American sisters led the radicalisation of the movement I was understanding the strength that emulates from connectedness within groups to develop confidence and creativity amongst children. The women's movement used the same process in consciousness-raising groups, a forum in which to exchange experiences. Although key figures emerged in the women's movement, it was apparent that leadership, rather than depending solely on charismatic figures, was evolving more organically. The consciousness-raising groups were the catalyst for personal narratives. The very process which alienated men was the bedrock of the strength that women could draw from each other. The landscape for women had altered irrevocably. The mass entry of women into the workforce and the Pill was changing our roles within the family. Our female voice emerged from collective support. By listening to stories of each other's lives in a safe environment we could make sense of our own. Personally it was a quest to find ourselves, politically it was formulating our campaigning for equality, abortion on demand, free childcare, equal pay.

I watched the separatists gather momentum attempting to exclude men from their lives. Men became angry. They scorned women's attention to detail and the personal, defining it as narcissistic. They were irritated by the personal gaze that women cast upon their own experience. Through talking we could draw attention from other women and from men, to the issues of gender equality.

I was thinking of my granny's gold and black cross-stitch tablecloth - embroidery. What, over the centuries had this women's work, dismissed as merely decorative, to tell us about women's lives and women's aspirations? Personal narrative led us to understand female marginalisation, acknowledge our dilemmas between maternal longing and professional calling. I of course had been observing since childhood, the strength my knitting aunties drew from each other.

Women who were participating in these consciousness-raising groups were primarily middle class, many graduates. I was an avid reader of Simone de Beauvoir who observed that women who were stuck in a poverty trap without access to opportunity through education, would forever be unable to take control in their lives. I knew, at that moment, I would apply the skills I was acquiring to access those areas of the community.

I also read Marilyn French's *The Women's Room*. Although set in America it expressed everything about the fifties I wanted to escape from. I also avidly read articles in *Spare Rib*, the first feminist magazine.

Germaine Greer's *The Female Eunuch* was published in1970. Greer, incorporated men into her world and wrote with passion about freedom and justice. She invited us to aspire, lead a life of equality, reach our full potential whilst still enjoying working alongside men. She was not a separatist.

In 1972 I had a series of conversations with Martha Stuart, an American film maker, who had made a series of films with women in the developing world entitled *Are you listening?* She was a pioneer. These figures led me, over the next fifty years, to work at grassroots level.

The feminist position for me did not come overnight, but slowly over time. I would struggle throughout my working life with strong male leadership. I sometimes despaired as women (including myself) instinctively took an acquiescent and subordinate role. I would, as I matured, increasingly turn to the wisdom and influence of female work colleagues and the continual evolving dialogue with female friends.

I'm researching hooped earrings at Camden Lock market wearing my cheesecloth maxi-dress, purple boots and a velvet cloak. I paint the rims under my eyes in thick kohl. Suddenly, shouting my name and waving frantically is Gillian Cohen, my friend from primary school. Her head is shaved and she wears a silver feminist symbol in one ear, dungarees and Doc Marten boots with the laces undone. She's carrying her baby in a papoose across her chest.

"Is it a girl?"

"Yes, thank goodness. I'm a separatist feminist now and I wouldn't be able to attend meetings with the baby if it was a boy."

"What's she called?" I ask as the smell of talcum powder reaches my nostrils as I kiss her.

"Blackberry."

Gillian had attended women-only conferences, listened to speakers tirading against men and been on reclaim-the-night marches, clasping her daughter against her chest.

"Oh, by the way, I'm a Quaker now."

I'm shocked. Why bother? I was relieved not to have time to think of religion. What would the calm of a Quaker meeting be like after the chanting and swaying and muttering in Hebrew that we had both watched in synagogue when we were little girls?

She shrugs. "It's good to be somewhere that's not angry." Does she mean the women on marches or her own Mum?

She invites me to attend a women's meeting in Tufnell Park saying "and bring a small mirror." She also persuades me to stop shaving my legs and armpits and to stop plucking my eyebrows.

When we arrive they are discussing Rosa Luxembourg. At least six of the women in the group are knitting the free pattern from Spare Rib magazine, a sweater with the women's movement symbol on the front.

Someone announces the session is called '*getting to know your own vagina*'. We are invited to sit round in a circle, each of us peering at our own genitalia. Gillian whips out her mirror and is soon concentrating. I am reluctant to start. Luckily Blackberry chooses that moment to start screaming.

"Don't worry," I leap up, "I'll take her outside." I grab the baby and run out of the session in relief. We both sit on a bench at the bus stop. Blackberry is now gazing up at me, deep in thought. I smile down at her.

"I'm not sure I want to know much more about my vagina," I whisper in her ear. "Would you?" She gurgles in reply, dribbling a little on her tightly clenched fist, which she shoves half into her mouth.

"I thought you'd agree, Blackberry, you are lucky, you don't have to think about all this for a long time." She chuckles, reaches for my thumb and pulls it towards her mouth.

The women I encountered in the arts collective as well as in women's consciousness-raising groups were usually graduates, working out a position on relationships and family. Monogamy was out of fashion and heterosexuality was also questioned. Some of the women who had married very young were now leaving their partners, choosing to live in all female collectives, often in short-term housing or squats.

This was our first flush of sexual freedom and autonomy. Because of the pill we could choose whether or not to have babies. Because of the strength women drew from the Movement, they started making choices about our lives without taking men into account. Women were pooling their time and financial resources; some went out to work and supported others who grew vegetables and minded the children. Single parenting would become a norm.

Some men now took care of the children and relinquished their career paths. Women often were starting theirs. These men watched their babies fight their way into the world. They were quietly committed to their families and found the opportunity of being involved with their children in a way not possible for their own fathers.

Other men had a different perspective on the liberation of contraception; it was no longer necessary to take responsibility and even ask the question whether sex was safe. It meant there never needed to be any discussion about commitment or responsibility. Sex became free and equal currency; men were off the hook.

Terry, a geology graduate from Leeds, worked with us on street shows, often playing the villain of the piece, the wicked Council Leader. He never quite knew where his young son, Tristan, and his mum were living. I used to watch him after the shows, digging into his pocket for change and ambling to the red phone box on the corner of the street. He was still in costume in his black cloak and bowler hat; he would be trying to call his son. If he managed to make contact we would sit in the van waiting for him for twenty minutes or half an hour while they chatted. He'd climb in the back of the van, tears pouring down his cheeks. Every week he felt he was losing his son a little more. Eventually he would calm down and sit in the back of the van knitting long, striped scarves for each of us. These scarves would see us through the long Yorkshire winters.

The Golden Vagina

I had visited Judy Chicago's installation *The Dinner Party*, when it came to London, a ceremonial banquet with vulva and butterfly motifs in the place settings.

I had attended art 'happenings' and watched performers making plaster casts of their own faces, breathing through straws up their noses, as they layered strips of plaster gauze dipped in water across their faces. Some performances went further with men making plaster casts of their penises and displaying them.

I rushed to the red call box on the corner of our street and phoned Gillian.

"I have a fantastic project. Come over to my place tonight and bring a take-away and a large pot of Vaseline." I bought strips of gauze impregnated with plaster. I arranged newspapers and the plastic tablecloth on the floor so the landlord wouldn't complain if we dripped plaster on his grubby carpet. A Rolling Stones album was playing when Gillian and Blackberry arrived. We ate her Indian takeaway, shared a bottle of wine and started work. My plan was to produce two unique plaster of paris vaginas, painted pure gold and exhibited, maybe at the Arts Lab, Drury Lane, where I watched happenings, chance music concerts and African poetry readings.

We lay back to back on the floor. Gillian had her legs up on the sofa. "All we need are stirrups," she murmured, "and it would be just like giving birth."

My legs were raised on the armchair, the backs of our heads were touching. I had prepared a tray for each of us, scissors for shaping the gauze strips, a yogurt pot of extra plaster and a jug of water in case we needed to supplement the chemist's supplies. We took great care to apply copious amounts of Vaseline to our genitalia (I had remembered this was an essential part of the process when once shown how to take a plaster mould of my hand).

"The plaster will just slide off when it's hard," she had said.

"I wonder what the shape will be like," Gillian said, as we layered the wet strips. I didn't answer I was concentrating on dabbing bits of plaster between the gauze strips and beginning to worry in case I would need to pee whilst the plaster was drying. I also remembered that urine slows down the drying process of plaster of Paris therefore I must not wet myself either. No jokes, our mood was turning serious. The newly opened bottle of wine was just out of my reach. Gillian was quiet now.

"Are you ok?"

"It's beginning to feel hot"

"Oh I forgot to tell you. Plaster always heats up whilst setting, don't worry, it'll cool down again in a second."

"OK, pass my glass".

I told her the bottle was out of reach. She shuffled across the room, on her backside and a great dollop of hardening plaster between her legs, reached out for the bottle that tipped, spilling wine, over her tee-shirt, face and my hair. We lay there laughing licking drips from our face and hair until the plaster was set.

I had imagined the plaster sculpture would just lift from our bodies in a perfect shape. Eventually we decided the plaster was set enough. We started to ease it away. Every few minutes we'd lie back exhausted with the effort before trying again.

"It won't loosen," I gasped, being tubbier than Gillian.

"Pull harder."

I tried, but had wedged the plaster so firmly in position it wouldn't budge. I tugged and heard Gillian's grunts of effort as she pulled at the set plaster as hard as she could.

"It's nearly off," she said eventually.

"Mine isn't."

I was close to tears now. Would we have to wait in casualty for five hours in this position? In front of other people? Would this need an operation?

Done it. Gillian had liberated her vagina. She came round to show me the flat oval shape with a slight indent in the middle, she was taking a large gulp of wine and putting a cushion under my head so I could drink too. I touched it cautiously.

"To think a baby came out of that tiny space," she said. I thought nothing is ever going to go in or come out of my tiny space again.

"Gillian, if I need an operation to remove this…."

"Don't be silly. You lie still and I'm going to pull."

"But then you'll see my bits."

"Well, it's a good job I've had a close look at my own so I know what I'm in for."

She started pulling.

Blackberry started crying.

I started crying.

Blackberry's cries got loud.

I started yelling with pain.

Gillian took a deep breath. Blackberry was screaming, I was screaming and the plaster was ripped off. Gillian's face was beetroot with effort. Mine was beetroot with pain. Blackberry's was beetroot with fury.

Gillian handed me my vagina and grabbed Blackberry, who started feeding. All went silent.

There were tears on my face. My legs were still on the sofa as I lay examining the ghastly object, oval like Gillian's but this had most of my black pubic hairs trapped and curled into the plaster. I got up slowly examining it.

"I'm not sure we can use these, what do you think?"

"You'd have to explain how we acquired them."

I watched Blackberry, calmly sucking, saucer eyes fixed on the object in my hands. Gillian started singing a lullaby, I joined in while blowing up my airbed and arranging my sleeping bag for Gillian's bed in front of the gas fire.

A long-stay psychiatric ward – Yorkshire 1969

This is a long stay mental hospital. It is a huge red brick Victorian building, opened in 1851, known across Europe as one of the *prestige institutions* to heal the human mind. It was overcrowded with poor sanitation. I visit with a volunteer, every Saturday afternoon to lead a creative writing session for a group of long-stay women. They have been incarcerated for many years, maybe through having an illegitimate baby, postnatal depression, unspecified mental illness.

We climb the stairs to a gloomy hall smelling of urine and polish. Only the tops of the trees are visible through the barred windows. We arrange the seats in a circle. Fifteen women are led in by a ward orderly in green overalls. They shuffle along in furry slippers, wearing stained baggy clothes. One or two sit together whispering; the rest are silent. A few start knitting. We play a word game to break the ice. It doesn't take long before most of the group are laughing and shouting out words, which I write on one side of the board. We start by asking for words about the season, then a sentence for the words that I write up on the other side. We hand out clipboards with paper and a pencil, inviting our participants to write down some of these sentences and make up new ones around the words that have been generated. They write eagerly. I listen to the scratching of pencils on paper. After a while we invite them to underline the bits they like, cross out what they decide to reject and redraft their poems on a fresh sheet. If they are happy, they read them out. Most of the group join in, proud to have an audience for their poems. We have all become poets.

We suggest they write more before next week's session and then we read out some poems to them: Philip Larkin, Keats, some children's poems, Sylvia Plath.

They say to me, "You read a poem." I feel shy, am startled when they applaud. The hour is up.

"You'll come again, won't you?" they ask, as we pull on our jackets. I marvelled how we had been able to support them to write with such assurance, using a combination of games, reading and writing. Their endeavours had been witnessed and respected by others. This had helped them re-connect with the parts of themselves lost through time, distant trauma and the sad monotony of their daily lives.

In two hours we had formed a community with those women. Words had knitted them together; they had celebrated each other. I recognised how their confidence grew slowly, every week, through writing together.

A short-stay psychiatric ward, Yorkshire 1974

Finally the nomadic life style exhausted me and I landed in a psychiatric ward.

I got to the point of slipping and sliding away from myself. I nearly lost who I was.

Maybe I had inhaled too much resin, too much cannabis, too many late nights listening to my friends playing music. I was losing sight of what my work was about; encounters of enchantment were elusive. Our lives were being diverted into political rhetoric. There was a struggle for survival, funding issues, organisational crises. There were some in our group of activists in Leeds who believed that the aim of our collective approach to the work and our own lives was the overthrow of capitalism.

I had been propelled by raw energy, developing the model and the support of Inter-Action London to initiate our programme. I had little interest in the political dialectic;

I wanted action. This was unacceptable to Marxist thinking. Eventually I had to leave Interplay, Leeds. I lost sight of myself as an animator and teacher; the others lost sight of me. The music had become too loud, there were no bars to rest between the notes. Action without reflection couldn't continue.

The sky went grey, heavy foreboding clouds, darkness.

Everything was too much; organising, remembering to have a shilling ready for the gas meter to light the gas fire or heat water to wash my hair.

I wanted to put down roots but couldn't reconcile this with my desire to fly, unclipped wings and the promise of our generation; anything else would be selling out. Maybe the silences in my childhood had congealed into a greasy lump somewhere in the middle of my chest and wouldn't move.

My parents' hostility also preyed heavily on my mind. I would phone their house from the red telephone box round the corner I still held their back door key and if there was no reply I crept home, opened the fridge door and devoured their cold dinner from last night, stuffing into my mouth with my fingers; I filled my coat pocket with apples.

No one ever said anything.

I tried a proper job in Yorkshire Television, as a researcher, pleased to earn proper money. I had a proper boyfriend, also earning real money, and we ate our tea together, every evening, in front of a colour television.

My boyfriend had two proper dogs, a chocolate and a cream Labrador. I would take them for long walks on the windy tops of Otley Chevin, climbing the rocks under a wild sky. He was still in love with his previous girlfriend and missed his children; his life was really at the other end of the telephone.

I sat on the floor half listening to his conversation, tickling the dogs' tummies, bored. Using a clean bathroom did not replace the magic encounters of the street. I was hooked on action; television felt like a diluted life and I wanted real encounters. I had already spent five years engaged in a process of community and I was unable to make the switch to documentary.

I am safe in here, in the hospital, behind the brick walls, on the bed and my feet don't quite touch the ground. My legs dangle over the side and I am clutching my backpack of belongings. My parents will arrive with an anxious look in their eyes, a wash bag, dressing gown and, if I'm lucky, some matjes herring.

I am instructed by a nurse to join the queue. I wait for my anti-depressants and receive instructions to swallow not chew as I am handed a glass of water. Then I have to open my mouth to show they have gone down and that I haven't saved them like a hamster in the pouches of my mouth to spit them out later.

I see my psychiatrist twice. He has ginger hair and is called Dr Sharp. He can't understand why anyone would want to be paid £7 a week to lead street processions for grubby children in deprived areas of Leeds. He is a man rising to the top of his career in adult mental health; he clearly agrees with my parents that any intelligent person ought to be doing the same. There is no counter-culture in his view, and where there is dissent there is ECT. There is no culture either; how can a song, a poem, a play written collaboratively lift the spirit and lead us to sanity? I am insane for trying. The grown-ups are against me.

The second time he sees me is two weeks later, I have dodged the cockroaches in the shower, finished *Lord of the Rings* and am half way through *The Women's Room* by Marilyn French.

I want to read and sleep.

I have watched patients mumbling to themselves, young girls with bandaged wrists and criss-crosses on their arms, patients fastened to their bed by broad rubber straps, a wedge of something pushed into their mouths to stop them biting their tongues, then wheeled down for ECT, electric currents through their brains to burn away the relentless depression consuming them.

The psychiatrist suggests the orderly takes me to the arts and crafts room. I obediently trot behind him as we twist and turn down the endless corridors. I can just see out of the tall windows and look at the grey sky and rows of northern red brick terraces that surround the hospital. I hear the groans and sighs of water travelling through the huge pea green pipes as we descend into the gloomy basement of this dilapidated Victorian building.

I sit down in the corner of the occupational therapy room, avoiding the willow whips soaking in the large sink ready for a new basket. A tiskit, a tasket.

I sing the little yellow basket song to myself in my head and hope the kindly bustling therapist won't decide I am a total basket case and cajole me into a basket weave. Suddenly I spot a pink ball of wool and a pair of knitting needles. While my fingers tease and pull the ball of wool, enjoying the feel of the yarn, I start counting up the garments my mother had knitted for me. I can chart the different transition points in my life through the garments she made. In OT, I reach out for the grey sock wool and start casting on. I laboriously create enough stitches on the needle to make a scarf and start, carefully checking at the end of each row that my stitches are even. I keep my head down and soon I am absorbed by the familiar rhythm of the needles. My hands have a life of their own; they know how to turn the knitting without needing to involve my aching brain. Everything suddenly seems ordered again, I am on safe, female territory; I have gone back to where I came from.

The light is fading in the OT room. I look up and am aware that everyone is shuffling around the room, shutting half-finished work into cupboards and draining water in the sink. Someone switches on the harsh fluorescent light, a signal to go back to the ward.

Knowing that knitting needles wouldn't be allowed upstairs, because I might stab someone else or even worse myself with a knitting needle, I wait until no one is looking and stuff the beginnings of my little grey scarf down my trousers. I hobble upstairs muttering, "I need the toilet."

I was eager to get to the toilet and settle on the closed lid with my knitting.

I concentrate my tongue out at the corner of my mouth as I loop the thread in front of the next stitch, then behind the next one, then in front again, until I have a row of moss stitch.

Later that week my father arrives to visit. He is looking around the ward, horrified. I sit on my bed, my head burrowed in Jack Kerouac's *On the Road*, pretending not to watch him. He is enraged, beads of sweat on his brow, he grabs me by the jacket and pulls me to my feet.

"What do you think you doing here? Why are you wasting your time, yourself? You have a choice, be what you want, get out there, I don't understand this playing on the street, I don't understand why you wear long black dresses. Why don't you care to earn any money? Don't make a mess of your life - you can choose what you can become, we couldn't. You have a bright light, it must not go out."

It's the only time I ever saw him cry.

"It must not go out, must not go out."

He was hitting me now and the nurse was looking anxious. He sank on to my bed, we both were wiping away snot with the backs of our hands. I reached under my pillow for my wibbly-wobbly scarf with too short fringing and put it round his neck.

I'm discharged and return home for Passover.

I sit next to my father during the Seder, everything is reassuringly as it's always been. I discard the black and wear navy blue corduroy hot pants, with a bib, violet tights and thigh-high, grey PVC boots, which my parents say make me look like a Berlin streetwalker. I tidy my hair and pin it up to please my father and watch him give thanks to God for leading the children of Israel out of captivity,

I now understand my father's dreams and hopes for me. I realise my inheritance from Europe and my responsibility for the lost souls. My father's guilt at surviving becomes the motivation for my own work.

Chapter 13

Milton Keynes – 1976

It is the heatwave summer of '76; we are a procession of performers, volunteers, children, parents and musicians, all wearing vivid costumes and carrying banners inviting children to follow. My hair is sprayed pink and I carry a wise woman's staff. We snake our way through a maze of new estates, crossing main roads, stopping at intervals to perform little vignettes.

My character is Professor Enid Prism, in possession of a hieroglyphic scroll that reveals the origins of Milton Keynes.

> *Prism the professor*
> *Became the proud possessor*
> *Of an ancient scrap of script*
> *In a creepy crawly crypt*

We appear like a band of troubadours from the middle ages, performing for the recent arrivals to the new town in the middle of the Buckinghamshire countryside. Our mission is community, to create a shared experience. This play invites children to spend their holiday creating a time capsule that will be buried in the ground. We explore how future generations might understand our new town through invented artefacts that we will leave behind. Together we will illustrate an account of our present lives and turn these accounts into stories for the future.

At the back of the procession is a rhythm cart, constructed out of an old pram chassis with wheels. Strapped to it are oil drums, pieces of metal, grates, grills, cymbals, found materials which when beaten send a cacophony of rhythms reverberating around the streets and across the fields. These are pounding through the streets, accompanied by saxophone, clarinets and an accordion. At intervals the bandleader blows his whistle, everything stops and when the procession is silent we burst into a verse of the song that presents the theme of our drama. Music was the heartbeat to evoke the spirit of Milton Keynes. Our orchestra is made of junk materials. It is music that opens its arms to embrace everyone. It is influenced by African drumbeats and Mexican mariachi on brass instruments, shepherds' pipes from Peru, the protest songs of Bob Dylan. We think fast, playing word games with the adolescents who are shouting comments on the street. We link arms and everyone dances, swinging partners round, stepping to the left, stepping to the right and eventually returning to the form of the circle.

Professor Prism reprises a theme of exploring the past, how the future will see us and how we create a sense of belonging for ourselves and each other in Milton Keynes. We were linking the lives of strangers through the magic of theatre.

> *Through spells and incantations*
> *She worked out the translations*
> *The key to all our dreams*
> *Is right here in Milton Keynes*

I become a listener – 1976

Sweet Sixteen

> *Happy birthday sweet sixteen*
> *Tonight's the night I've waited for*
> *Because you're not a baby any more*
> Sedaka and Greenfield 1961

A whole housing estate could all start listening to each other. As in Peter Cheeseman's documentaries, I visualised excavating the stories from life, the stories within an individual's experience.

I thought less of external themes, more of transition points in our personal lives that punctuate the life cycle.

Young people ask questions and then listen to older people's stories. They made a video, a performance or artwork to be viewed by everyone. When an audience gathers together to watch, listen and witness these stories we become a community. Dig where you stand, start where you are, talk to each other, explore meaning and light up the stories, create something new together. Create alchemy between action and memory.

I chose the theme *Sweet Sixteen*, because it represents a period of transition and rebellion. We become our own person at sixteen, leaving our parents beliefs behind. We reach a moment of change, a cusp between leaving childhood and stepping into adulthood. Teenagers were curious to meet us as teenagers.

As memories poured out they were turned into weekly street newspapers, hand-drawn on coloured carbons and printed off on an old Gestetner duplicator from the boot of a car. Stories were presented in Polaroid photographs, exhibited at weekly street parties with cakes, sandwiches, and pop for the children, cups of tea for adults. Elvis records blasted out from a record player. Residents jived on the street. We emerged from the hairdresser's booth modelling beehives, looking like Helen Shapiro singing *Walking Back to Happiness*.

We sat indoors, making videos of each other's stories. There were grannies and parents of teenagers and little ones. Someone said "Oh, I was a nippy at Lyons corner house," and then someone else said "I remember, we'd go dancing to the Hackney Empire and then the sirens would go off." The stories gathered momentum and four hundred people attended the finale of music and demonstrations of dancing through the ages, in full period costume.

Young people stepped into someone else's shoes and saw the world differently. Maybe for these people, who'd migrated from London or Glasgow to Milton Keynes, we were creating a history of the residents, and community through shared stories and collaboration.

"People kept coming, when we did video sessions in people's living- rooms. They were packed and when we did the cabaret at the end there were 400 people in the audience. There were always fifty kids ready to do a newspaper, smiles on people's faces. A joy, that's the only way that I can say, maybe there was some value in it."

A volunteer

Things that mother never told us

MILTON KEYNES
EXPRESS

FRIDAY, SEPTEMBER 9, 1977

Sweet Sixteen
Trip back down old memory lane

NOSTALGIA, cabaret and magic attracted crowds to Beanhill's small meeting place on Friday.

Most people on the estate must have turned out to watch the finale of the Sweet 16 project which has taken the school holidays to complete.

A team of Inter-Action workers roamed the estate and asked mums and dads what they could remember about the glorious age.

Then they wrote songs and organised games based on the information they had gained for weekly street parties.

Friday's gathering was the culmination of it all. A small stage was erected and the building was decorated with cardboard puppets and palm trees by designer Liz Hawkins.

A buffet, soft drinks — and the alcoholic variety — were also arranged.

Teddy boys chatted up the girls with beehive hairstyles and the show included rock 'n' roll records and some magic.

Three members of the audience chose playing cards from entertainer Charlie Stafford and to their amazement all three were correctly guessed by Steve Ley. Steve later turned fire-eater while Milton Keynes musician Paul Swannell gave a roll on the drums.

The next act was a bit of extra-sensory perception performed by the beguiling — and well disguised — Madame Gummskaya (Carolyn Gurney).

It was also magic to watch the delicate feet of the Darrel Dancers as they moved to the music of their mothers' era.

Tuneful Maggie Daly, of Beanhill, sang some nostalgic singalong songs which warmed the hearts of many of the older people.

The whole evening organised with the usual enthusiasm of Inter-Action was like a big party enjoyed by young and old alike.

A Previous street party on Beanhill.

Preparing for the Cabaret.

Sweet Sixteen
Milton Keynes

Video and Cable – 1977-78

Turn the idea of celebrity on its head, exploit the mystery and use 'television' as a tool for narrating personal stories. I was very interested in how we could take control of the media. In 1969 I filmed women and their babies with a discarded camera from Yorkshire Television, so large it was delivered in a van. After that came cardboard cameras and storyboarding children's drama on play sites.

I was excited by Channel 40, Milton Keynes' experiment in Community Cable Television. Citizens were in charge of their own reporting. I often thought about the young mums in the new town. What is it like to be a woman alone living on an estate with a baby or toddler? There was an inadequate transport system, no city centre, no natural meeting places. Video could be the way of linking the lives of isolated women by taking the 'Personal is Political' approach out of their living-rooms and onto the television screens of Milton Keynes.

We created *Things that Mother Never Told us*, a series of programmes by and for local women. This project challenged traditional approaches to documentary, using external reportage worked collaboratively from within the group. The programmes were largely edited by the women themselves. I initiated the project by informally connecting with mothers whom I had met on play sites and filmed in their living rooms.

In an interview recorded in 1977 one of the women, Sue, described some of the themes and also how we managed the technical process:

"What came out of our first tape was mainly conflicts with authority, even going out of our houses, wrangles with the Milton Keynes development corporation, with doctors and teachers; and how difficult it is when we're us and they're them.

We then returned to Channel 40 and used their big editing suite. We had to sit through a good hour of tapes and say: 'What are the main points of discussion? What themes came out of it? What do we want used and what do we want cut out?' We learned about logging and editing and then we decided to learn how to film ourselves."

Moving again

Settling in Milton Keynes seemed like the secondary school in Leeds. Yet again I felt the impulse to move, work elsewhere, follow different dreams. I worked with young Mexican-American women in California using video. They were beautiful adolescents, at the same time as being sophisticated young mothers. Some made detailed pencil drawings of faces. They made videos of their drawings, their own faces, their little children's faces and voice over commentaries about living in Los Angeles, about their dreams, their fears of speaking English with an accent and hopes and wishes for their children. They were unemployed living in back streets looking after their babies. They showed their tapes in the local community centre. The hall was crowded, their families were there, their men. There was music and singing and thunderous applause at the end. They had been talking about their lives now and their hopes for the future - la Nueva Chicana! The new Mexican woman.

Then I come home, I start creating a home. I land in London

The Owl and the Pussycat – Milton Keynes 1975

A girl sits on the back step blowing soap bubbles. The bubble grows stronger each time. A giant sphere balances in space. She is transfixed by the colours trapped inside. It wobbles and then slowly floats away. She spreads her wings, lifts off and follows.

She hovers like a kestrel, over the sleeping city. She is mesmerised by the ribbons of light, her soap bubbles, , snow trapped inside the snowstorm ball, tiny wind up dancing ballerina on musical boxes and the whizzing spinning tops made of painted tin. She sees them all as she flies past windows with no curtains. She is looking at the treasures of strangers.

Lying in a walnut shell is a perfect baby. It is blowing a dandelion clock, a soft whisper and the fluttering of air against her cheek.

It gurgles, for Zero's tiniest soap bubble is as big as the universe. The baby is lying on her back watching the clouds racing, 'Look, look' and points at a black shape against the blue sky eager to join the flying bird .

Silence is broken by the clatter of lids as dustbins are overturned. She watches the wild boar, frantic chewing of hungry tusked creatures. Somewhere a fox forages in the city's waste for breakfast to feed its hidden hungry cubs.

It hesitates by the letterbox as if about to post a letter to his cousin at that moment lurking by the chicken shed at the edge of the forest. A plumper fox, salivating as feathered bodies shift on warm straw.

The caramel dog lifts his head at the sound of birds' wings flapping. Zero returns to the back step, and folds her wings.

She reaches her hand into the straw and stands holding the still warm egg against her cheek.

PART FIVE

Little Voice

Chapter 14

The end of an era

*I think we've been through a period where too many
people have been given to understand that if they
have a problem, it's the government's job to cope
with it. "I have a problem, I'll get a grant."... you
know, there is no such thing as society..... People have
got the entitlements too much in mind, without the
obligations....*
Margaret Thatcher, 1987

1979 was the twilight of the radical arts movement; Labour lost
the election and Margaret Thatcher became Prime Minister.
She was to challenge what she saw as a national expectation of
entitlement without personal effort.

She had devolved control of the Greater London Council's
(GLC) by 1986 and abolished the Inner London Education
Authority (ILEA) by 1990 because their socialist policies were
in conflict with her vision.

My last project with Inter-Action was initiating a sculpture
and planting project to improve an infant school playground.
An environmental and sustainability movement was emerging
in primary education that included building outdoor
classrooms, initiating vegetable planting and encouraging
plant and insect presence in the school environment.

The children have designed a concrete jungle with exotic
plants and ferocious animals. Each class arrives, dressed in

old shirts, carrying trowels. Femi, from Sierra Leone, is five. He says little and, when he does speak, understanding him presents a challenge. He has just been taken into care; his parents have disappeared. He stands alone in the playground, lost, confused. I kneel next to him and start showing him pictures of animals. At first he shies away from me but as I put the brightly coloured cards on the ground he slowly becomes interested. We run holding hands to the long, playground wall and hold the animal pictures against it. I am trying to communicate that we are designing a relief mural. Then I point at the coloured pots of paint waiting. He's very serious as he follows my finger with his eyes. I do a silly mime of different creatures, after each one pointing questioningly at him. He is slowly beginning to smile. Suddenly he takes a piece of chalk and draws a lion on the floor. When he's finished he pats himself on the chest proudly.

"Aha, a lion. So you're a lion?" He nods and runs over to the wall.

"Lion on wall," he says running back to me.

"Yes, yes. Where would you like your lion to go?" He chalks the spot and together we copy his lion, soon there are several parents helping him add it to the class mural.

I was preoccupied by Femi, thinking about the individual care he needed from all adults on the site. Many of those five year olds clutching their trowels and designing their mural needed emotional support.

Ten years earlier ILEA's drama panel had approved Inter-Action's innovative work on the use and application of the games for social and educational purposes, now the withdrawal of support meant there were diminishing opportunities for artists, activists and experimental educators. We were no longer activists of the street but applying our work to the classroom. Work, which had been edgy and experimental during the previous decades, was becoming integrated into mainstream practice.

The rear end of an elephant

Seventy per cent of the children in a school in Tower Hamlets were originally from Sylhet, a region in Bangladesh. The head teacher, concerned about how to integrate these children, received an ILEA grant to develop activities and invited Inter-Action to the school. This was another initiative that would be halted by government cuts.

We lead games sessions in pairs, and share responsibility, demonstrating co-operation and mutual respect. In Tower Hamlets David[5] and I show each game rather than simply describe it. We make the children laugh; they make us laugh.

In one game we are all modelling each other into the shape of a large elephant. David is at the front with a group of children forming a trunk, I am in the middle, forming the body. A woman stands watching from the doorway. A small boy is kicking a chair. The woman holds his arm and encourages him towards the swaying elephant, she bends down, forming the rear end with the boy on her back as the tail.

"Hello," she says introducing herself through David's legs. "I'm Marjorie."

In 1970, Marjorie Boxall was an educational psychologist working within ILEA. Hers was a lone, determined voice preoccupied with the needs of young children who found difficulty coping with early school experiences. To improve their life chances she was emphatic that they needed to be taken back to much earlier infant nurturing for a condensed period. That involved creating a safe environment, a room in the school that had an intimate domestic feel with soft furnishings, a small kitchen, bright colours and grownups with arms outstretched and love in their hearts. This concept of catching up developmental milestones within a caring environment is now generally accepted.

Marjorie worked tirelessly within the ILEA to integrate Nurture Groups into the school system. She was tolerated by the authorities but never allowed to become a driving force within the system. Her Nurture Groups were established because several   head teachers were seeing positive results

5 - David Powell was a director of the Inter-Action from 1971 to 1985. The company he subsequently formed, DPA Ltd. worked nationally and internationally on research animation and project development in the field of community arts. This included planning for twenty years of Lottery investment in the North; and supporting local artists and producers connected with London's Olympic project. His research is currently focused on rebalancing public funding for arts and culture between London and the rest of the country.

and so lobbied the ILEA to keep them open. Nurture took place in small groups and the young children were at the same time learning essential social skills such as turn-taking, sequencing actions and listening skills. Marjorie had initiated and successfully implemented nurture rooms in around fifty ILEA schools.

After our elephant encounter Marjorie guided me on a tour of Nurture Groups. We travelled together across London in pouring rain, Marjorie explaining psychoanalytic theories on infancy as we stepped on and off buses. Like drowned rats we fell into the Nurture Rooms soaking wet. The children, with help from the classroom assistant, made us toast and tea, served in red plastic mugs.

They sit on cushions around us, climb on and off our knees, offer warm biscuits fresh from the oven. We chat, we tell stories about the rain, using Marjorie's dripping umbrella. It's as cosy as afternoon tea with knitting aunties. I want to stay.

David Powell – Game session 1981

Sculpting an elephant - 1981

Nurture Groups

> *Create the world of earliest childhood in school, and*
> *through this build in the basic and essential learning*
> *experiences normally gained in the first three years,*
> *and so enable the children to participate fully in*
> *the mainstream class, typically within a year. The*
> *process is modelled on normal development from*
> *birth... and the content is the essential precursor of*
> *established foundation stage education for three to*
> *five-year-olds.*
> Marjorie Boxall: Nurture Groups in School (2002)

After Stephen Joseph and ED Berman, Marjorie was my
third teacher. I was drawn to her compassion and her tireless
campaigning on behalf of nurture groups. I recognised that,
as a psychologist, she spoke a language and held a map within
her head. She worked from a theoretical base which I lacked.

The cosy bright rooms with soft surfaces and toys were
designed for very young children. Marjorie showed me how
basic nurturing routines were essential for healthy, early

development: breakfast, taking turns to lift toast from the plate, telling each other about that morning, the journey to school, discussing the colour of the leaves and how they whipped around our legs on the pavement. She invited me to use the games that she had witnessed on the elephant day. She saw how they taught children socialization skills; listening, an awareness of a dance of dialogue, building on each other's ideas, changing tone of voice.

Together we created a curriculum and formulated a series of activities. We field-tested our ideas across schools in London.

What did I need to understand about children unable to settle in the classroom and therefore challenging to the education system? I had a teacher's number so I could be a teacher again. I needed my own nurture group.

In the school corridor crouches a neat figure with dark hair, wearing blue shorts and matching striped t-shirt. He is arranging his paintings on the floor. The nurture group is curating an art exhibition.

I kneel.

"Hi," I say. "I like your picture."

He glances at me.

"I have to write my name 'cos it's going on the wall."

"Do you want some help?"

He nods.

"Can you write the first letter?" I ask, edging a bit closer.

He laboriously writes a big P in the corner.

"Your name starts with "P", let me guess what it is…."

He's now slowly shaping an A. He can't wait for me to guess.

"My name is Pablo," he says, looking up with shining eyes.

"Pablo," I repeat.

The decision is made; I start teaching on Monday.

Through Paul I learn about the pain and distress in children who lose their way and need help to find confidence to learn. I learn how every little building brick can help mend the fissures in their lives. Even when he starts secondary school Paul still returns to read *Where the Wild Things Are* to the nurture children. He sits, in his pristine blue blazer, gravely showing each illustration, still a little boy reading to even littler boys.

I am on playground duty again blowing my whistle to catch the attention of children swirling around in the storm, giddy with the wind and swept along with the autumn leaves.

I am in a classroom again, sixteen years later, a nurture teacher with arms outstretched.

The children were five and six years old, many had stepped into the classroom from a home life of chaos. Marjorie and I were collaborating in writing a curriculum of knitting, cooking, baking and country dancing, teaching the right from the left, steps this way and that, making patterns with our bodies, creating a routine, a familiar life, safe and predictable.

They baked bread squeezing and kneading the dough, laughing and singing. We cooked jacket potatoes and grated cheese on a Baby Belling stove with two rings in the classroom. Several mums appeared at the classroom door asking for the recipe; we sent home an illustrated recipe sheet every week, in several languages. The mothers come to chat about their cooking. Sometimes we cooked together. The intimacy of the nurture room was anchoring my own work; I was working less with the children, increasingly with the parents.

I was also a mum now, I liked chatting. It was my life too.

The little girl who won't speak whispers her secrets in the ear of my dog. Cobweb sits quietly receiving pats, hugs and squeezes all afternoon. She listens to the whispers of the child refusing to talk. Blonde hair falls over Cobweb's head as the child sits with her arms around his neck whispering in his ear. He never betrays her confidences, just gives her a gentle lick and hopes for a biscuit. The little girl knows Cobweb loves her, because every week when we walk on Hampstead Heath he chooses her, running alongside and chasing after the sticks she throws. Sometimes she forgets herself and runs ahead shouting "Cobweb, I'm here, I can run faster than you." She can't of course, but the wise dog lets her pretend. Only a dog, but he did his best.

Back indoors and sitting round the table for tea and the biscuits baked that morning, children take turns saying what they liked about the walk on the Heath, pulling acorns out of their pockets, sharing their treasures. They draw pictures of their walk. They write a sentence underneath. Months pass and their drawings and writings become a book.

The Times they were a changin'

The time had come to put away the hooped earrings, and to cut the knotted hair. I was now a single parent putting bread on the table and buying roller skates. I still encouraged the children in our neighbourhood to dip their feet in buckets of paint and run along rolls of newsprint. At school we had now entered a world of prepared lesson plans in tried and tested manuals, parenting programmes from the US and pristine art materials sold in expensive blister-packs. Until then I had been a foot soldier, my hands in the baking bowl, and in the paint pot. Now, it was time, even for me, to join the professionals and become an expert. At the same time the National Curriculum had become the main focus of primary education. Every walk, every biscuit needed an explanation in terms of key stages. Our programme had to fit into a box of English comprehension or maths. I spent more time writing up my week in the nurture group in national curriculum terms, than I spent preparing my lessons for the class.

I was also simplifying the activities. I realised we were dancing less, taking fewer walks outside, more sitting down at desks; the only way I could fit in the weekly demands of the curriculum.

Children living behind cracked windows, and boarded up doors were emerging from the shadows. The children of drug addicts, the children of desperate asylum seekers, the children of trafficked women. I found them in the corners of the playground, behind the curtains of the school hall. They were silent and untrusting suspicious, or kicking the furniture, kicking me, kicking the world which had betrayed them. I encouraged and cajoled but often could not reach them. I knew they needed pre-work, before they could even access the nurture group.

I understood the help they needed was beyond modifying their behaviour. These children, shivering on the margins, needed capturing before their hearts hardened and their brains atrophied with consequences of crime and delinquency ahead. Their outside life needed mending before their inner life had a chance. I instinctively recognised that change could only take place within a relational context, taking into account the circumstances around the child, the external landscape as well as the internal landscape. I decided to retrain. I chose systemic psychotherapy as my therapeutic model.

I resolved to train as a psychotherapist before I would be forever trapped in a dying arts movement, or be forced to earn my living in an increasingly narrow education system.

Chapter 15

I become a psychotherapist

> *Every human existence is a life in search of a narrative...When someone asks you who you are, you tell your story. That is, you recount your present condition in the light of past memories and future anticipations. You interpret where you are now in terms of where you have come from and where you are going to.*
> Richard Kearney (2002)

I drive past Big Ben on my way to Vauxhall and a day's training ahead. I have handed over the responsibility to my tutors for the ideas in my head. I will spend four years of not initiating but integrating, absorbing and discovering ideas, slowly turning them into practice. I re-train alongside women who have raised their children in nuclear, blended, reconstituted or step-families. Some have families across the seas. These women have spent twenty-five years cooking tea and are now stepping out of the kitchen. We lend each other papers, read each other's essays, help each other through our exams. For four years I buy salami and cheese sandwiches at the Portuguese deli every Thursday afternoon.

We are taught in teams, for me a continuation of the collaborative work of the seventies. A tutor sits behind a screen watching our conversations with clients.

As I enter the world of therapy, fifteen years after the second wave of feminism, I am aware that the profession is mainly led by men, charismatic leaders, whose training workshops are crammed full of women. Not much change here, the wise women stay in the consulting room, offer advice behind a screen, lead from the back in soft voices.

Preparing for exams, I am video-editing tiny bits of tape where there is a question, a response, a moment of encounter, when things change in the therapy room. I trawl through videotaped sessions to assemble these moments. They will be explained to examiners who will invite me to shine a spotlight on a particular theory and its relevance to my practice. Before exams there is a frenzy of preparation, a viva, a video, a dissertation - all within a few weeks of each other.

I see clients every week, earning a living and cooking dinner. My Mum comes down from Leeds to fetch my son from school. This learning was precious in middle age; it was a metamorphosis.

Post training

> *Between stimulus and response, there is a space. In*
> *that space is our power to choose our response. In our*
> *response lies our growth and our freedom.*
> Viktor E Frankl – Man's Search for Meaning

I emerged after four years a systemic psychotherapist, poring over new theoretical maps whilst embarking on conversations through the jungles of human experience. My maps would underpin questions about relationships within families, forming an arc from the past to the future, identifying family patterns and narratives that pass through generations. Maps would shape questions about context and circumstances, the life cycle, birth to death, dreams to divorce. My maps would lead me and my clients in an exploration of hidden beliefs, conventions and phrases, illuminating dark and dusty corners of lives held in place by obsolete cultural beliefs, religion, family rules and national oppression.

From the Icelandic Sagas, stories written on bark and eaten in midwinter when fuel ran short, to a text on a smartphone, we have narrated the many layers of our lives so that others may understand us. It's how we make sense of who we are, reminding our listeners we have many parts and multiple contexts and ways of being.

My diploma licensed me to earn my living listening and responding to stories. The territory was the clients sitting before me.

I was serving my apprenticeship to become a psychotherapist, in the circular narration of stories and questions. Again I am listening to stories. We can't change what is behind us but we can shape what is before us and how we think about it.

I decide to begin at the beginning, to work with mothers and babies.

1992 - Baby's First Year - Patterns for a Lifetime

> *Sweet mother I no go forget you*
> *for the suffer wey you suffer for me.*
>
> *Sweet mother I no go forget you*
> *for the suffer wey you suffer for me.*
>
> *When I dey cry, my mother go carry me--she go say,*
> *'my pikin', wetin you dey cry ye, ye,*
> *stop stop, stop stop make you no cry again oh.*

Traditional West African lullaby sung in group each week before eating. (Sweet mother 1976)

I stand in the candlelit room in Minneapolis, Minnesota watching young women rubbing massage oil into their hands as they kneel before their babies who are lying on fluffy towels. These women have experienced abusive, damaged lives. Their hands are asking permission from their babies to touch. The leader instructs them gently. Some mothers are able to meet the baby's gaze, some find the invitation to intimacy too frightening and turn their heads away. Others start humming a lullaby, as their hands slide over the little bodies; someone remembers the words and others join in. They sing together.

I am watching a life-changing moment; a new baby has the power to create a new story. A new life means a fresh relationship, no stigma attached.

The baby understands its world through its body; how it is kept warm, how it is given milk, how it is held, how it is changed.

The mother uses both her own body and her soul to give her baby love in a way that makes it feel safe and comforted.

Vulnerable mothers need support and I long to create a community around the mother and baby relationship, by talking, photographing, writing, creating videos of magic moments and celebrating both the baby and the mothers' endeavour.

When I become a qualified family therapist in the public health service (NHS) I am able to do this thirteen years later. My clinical training helps me understand neuroscience research, the baby's brain during its first year of life and the chilling consequences if its emotional needs are not met.

The programme was called *Baby's First Year; patterns for a lifetime.*[6]

Mothers learned to trust the relationships they were building through conversations, through words, through touch, baby massage, through playing on the seashore, and, as I knew so well from my own early years and from nurture groups, cooking and eating together,

The babies watched, waited, creating their poems of sounds and smiles and dances with wriggling bodies and waving limbs with their Mums. The vulnerable young mothers had faced many difficulties such as post-natal depression and marginalisation but they all wanted the best for their babies and here was an opportunity for a new start

----

6 - The programme was adapted from Project STEEP (Steps Toward Effective Enjoyable Parenting), an intervention developed in the United States in response to a study implemented in 1975, The Parent Child Project, by Egeland, Deinard and Stroufe. They were asking: What allows some children to develop into healthy competent people even though they grow up in especially challenging environments? The results from their programme involving 75 at risk families with a control group of 83 showed that mothers became more sensitive to their babies and were more realistic about their capabilities. Families coped better with stressful life events; children socialised more easily; and performed better in school.

Here are some comments from the young mothers before their babies were born:

"I want to do the best for my baby." Tracey

"I want him to have a better start than I had." Loren

"I want to be able to understand what she wants." Hilary

"I'd be pleased for any help I can get, my own Mum isn't well enough." Charlene

"I need to watch others to help me do it right." Suzette

They regularly wrote about their experiences with their children. Each mum sat close to her baby, she wrote in her own voice and in the baby's voice about their lives together.

I'm never bored anymore
I look at you like there's no tomorrow
Watching your smile
Playing and singing to you
Watching you grow day by day
When I feed you, you hold on to the bottle like you're feeding yourself
You have given a purpose to my life
We went to the seaside and I paddled in the sea
The sand was all soft and squelchy in my hands like mud
I enjoyed the fish and chips too
I like my Mummy massaging me because it feels soft and her hands are really gentle;
Me and my Mum got to be very close.
I love the feel of oil on my Mummy's hands as its all warm and slippery and makes me feel safe and loved.

Showing and expressing love was at the heart of the work. Through their writing they understood how the babies expressed their love. They used their poems to reflect the depth of emotion in the relationships with their baby

We created a community around the mothers and babies. They held an exhibition of their writing and photographs in the community centre.

> *Just looking at the photos and reading the*
> *scripts made me think about what my mother*
> *meant to me and how I want to be remembered*
> *by my own children. It's a beautiful display*
> Visitor to exhibition.

These young women witnessed each other being good mothers and their community celebrated them..

Together we all created a community of love.

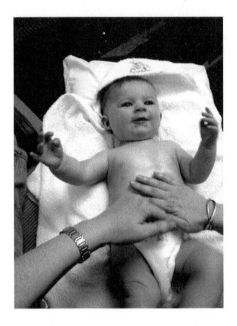

Conversations and communities

I am working in a Sheffield child and adolescent mental health clinic, part of the National Health Service. I work alongside clinicians motivated by change, fighting against tides of poverty and inequality. A multi-disciplinary team means there is an ever-changing kaleidoscope of theoretical perspectives from the different professional positions. Our common aim was to help repair the lives of children. When we met with the families we each looked for different signs and our work had a different focus.

The building is intimate and friendly, clean comfortable rooms, armchairs and John Lewis curtains. We eat our lunch together discussing our cases, our walks in the Peak District and our worries about the future of the NHS. I arrive at the weekly Friday morning meeting clutching my steaming coffee, eagerly anticipating the case presentation and ensuing discussion.

Exploratory Laporotomy

> *A new doctor works at our clinic;*
> *Quick off the mark, a sharp tongue,*

Penetrating Indian gaze.
She confuses me with her jeans and shirts one
day,
Flowing saris the next.
"How does she decide in the morning? I think,
How does she decide who she wants to be
When she wakes up?"
Gets her son ready for school.
When does she choose the necklaces?
The shoes, the colours of the day?
The reds, burnt oranges,
The green with delicate embroidery,
The white and black patterned to infinity.

We talked about cameras;
She knows the apertures and shutter speeds
And mega pixels;
How to take pictures in the dead of night
And in the light of day.

She met one of my families once, by chance.
I was ill and she was there, available, on duty.
"I did an exploratory laparotomy" she said
"A what?"
"It's when you open up the tummy.
The patient hurts you see, and you don't
understand...
You open up the tummy and you feel around.
You are exploring. Maybe you find, maybe you
don't,
The cause of this pain,
The invisible hurting inside,
The place where the patient has pointed.
There it is, that's where it hurts so I feel around,
Prodding, exploring, invading"

This vibrant Indian doctor and I prodded together, investigated and explored the cause of the pain. We pondered the invisible hurting inside. We searched where the patient had pointed, sometimes we saw them getting better, often we never knew. Conversations in the therapy room were encounters. We listened carefully to a story owned by the narrator, watched the flickers of expression on the face. They were invited to search for a new story, maybe with new characters or a new script, to find a new way of looking at the world. Together we find a new story.

At first I was fearful of what I didn't know, I struggled with the different models. However, through discussion, collaboration and listening to Friday case descriptions my mind was opening space for disciplines and ideas that were far beyond my tiny pool of knowledge. I slowly looked for similarities, ways to make connections, rather than looking at the differences that separated us. We talked about our roles as observers of families; how parents sometimes gathered their strength to shape a new path, and other parents sat with depleted energy waiting for us to make new sense of old stories. We stood between the different worlds, different characters, managing different feelings.

How I worked

I asked a child and his parents about school, the family and circle of friends, to build a picture of his life. We needed to go beyond today's specific worries. I listened to parents' problem stories whilst waiting for an opportunity to change the conversations. My hope was for parents to reconnect with the magic of their child. Then, the child would see himself in a different light. I encouraged conversations about the good experiences and positive moments together.

The children usually listen attentively to their parents' stories, wondering whether they are still loved, whether they are good enough to love. They are eager to participate in a conversation, to express themselves in their own way.

We were all *in this together*.

259

The Mango Tree

The little girl draws a map showing her grandmother's house, her yard and the walk across the field. I ask her what is in the yard. She answers smiling.

"A mango tree, we played under it when it was too sunny and my grandma sang to us." She was still smiling as a tear rolled down her cheek.

"I remember the mango tree," said her mother. "We sat under it in the hot sun too. Oh, how I miss it." She puts her arm round the girl, picks up a crayon and starts to draw the mango tree. They draw together, mother and daughter, for a long time, sharing coloured crayons, humming a tune the grandmother had sung for them many times.

The rabbits

Mum doesn't speak English. The children do but choose to ignore me. I sit quietly whilst these two little refugee sisters play with farmyard animals, building bigger and bigger fences around them. They are like two small chirruping sparrows, heads close together as they debate which animal was the mother, which animal would protect the babies and who is the enemy. I remark on the strength of the fences as I sit on the floor with them, waiting, with pencil and paper.

One points at the paper. "Write down," she says imperiously. She tells me about the foxes at the end of the garden. "They come when you're asleep they come when mother is not there. The foxes always come for the rabbits."

"How many rabbits?"

"Two of course," the smaller sister whispers, creeping closer. "We have two rabbits in a hutch, with straw they are very cosy, mother feeds them, they live close to the back of our house but the foxes will come at night when it's dark and everyone is asleep. I lie in bed listening for their steps on the path."

"Me too," adds the little one, wide-eyed.

"The mother, she keeps moving the rabbits so the foxes won't find them." They shuffle the animals around a tiny space.

The next week, they are building more fences.

"Where is the story we wrote last week?

I place it in front of them.

"Sometimes you see a moon at night and hear trees whispering and then you can see the foxes coming for the rabbits."

"Big teeth," the little one adds.

"But the mother has moved the rabbits again."

We repeat this story over several weeks.

I didn't know if this family kept rabbits. I didn't know if there were foxes on the local housing estate. I did know they have a pale and worried mother, who speaks little English. I am witnessing a description of these children's experiences, their fear and their trust in the mother who led them to safety. One day they stop building the fences and spread out the baby animals over the rug.

"What's happening?" I ask.

"Oh its summer now, they're having a holiday."

"And the rabbits?"

"They're playing in the sunshine too. Did you know rabbits hop when they're happy?"

The little girls in their rabbit story built fences over and over until it was safe enough to hop in the open grass again.

THE MOTOR CAR MONSTERS WHO ARE SPOILING MY LIFE

Frightening

Scared

Jumpy

Working on the edge

I work with teenagers, pulling them back from the edge. Hollow desperate eyes, bandaged wrists, sullen faces, bleached blonde hair and the mask of eye shadow, slick of lipstick; body piercing and glittering navels. Fragile teenagers.

We have a little rescue dog, a fluffy creature, curly tail and terrible teeth. She barks like a banshee and runs, blazing a sniffing trail through the Peak District. She always runs straight to the edge, the furthest boundary scratching and clawing her way through the wire fence, thicket hedge and barricades to seek her freedom. Sometimes she hurls herself against any obstacle standing in her way, sometimes she persistently searches until there is a hole to squeeze through, a weakness in the structure, so that she can burrow a hole for herself and slip underneath.

We are never quite sure where she goes, when she reaches the other side. She might disappear at great speed into dark undergrowth, and a quiver of bracken leaf tells us where she is passing through. Other times she runs at trees barking, looking up at their branches watching the movement of a distant leaping squirrel. She might simply stand motionless, unsure of what to do next, waiting for signal from a world we can't see smell or hear.

Our job is to stand waiting, calling, offering treats in loud clear voices, feigning cheerfulness, giving her confidence over great distances, reminding her where we are, where she can return, that we are standing in the rain, waiting.

Working with a Kosovan refugee family

> *In dialogue, a person is present to another (and the other), they are attentive and aware - listening and waiting. In the stillness of this "in-between world" they may encounter what cannot yet be put into words...*
> Martin Buber 1947

They arrive with their neighbour who already speaks English and acts as interpreter. They are a bedraggled little family, the girl with nightmares, sleepwalking trying to turn the key in the lock, eyes wide open. Mum has shut down, she strings three words of English together to voice her despair. She describes her dreams of fighting in the street, of bloodshed; a tiny girl carried in her mother's arms to a foreign country, a strange language and a hostile reception from fierce officials.

The father had arrived here first, grabbed by the police on arrival, pushed through doors and on to buses taking him to this bleak northern city in November sleet, mist shrouding the surrounding hills. He tells me about the detention centre; he was so afraid. He thought they'd send him back, alone, not realising his babies were here with their mother in the damp flat with dripping walls. He has no papers. They tell him he will have to go to London to get his papers, how would he pay for the fare? Could he walk?

Then he had stood in front of the stern headmistress in his shabby jumble sale coat shivering, trying to remember his daughter's birthday, her age, closing his eyes to conjure up her solemn little face. He was so nervous his mind went blank; he could hardly remember a word of English. He'd got it wrong, all wrong, and now she has to change classes because she's the wrong age in the wrong group and doesn't really want to leave her friends in the other class. Maybe it doesn't matter anyway because they've got papers from the Home Office now and they will move house, they might move right away and then she won't see her friends again anyway, just like she didn't see her granny again, or her aunty or anyone else she can't now remember all that time ago in Kosovo.

The little girl dreamt she was holding a light in her two hands, a light that would stop the fighting, that would make everyone happy again. She stands in the middle of the room, her mum, her good neighbour and I watch her cup her hands to contain this precious light of hope, her face is glowing as she holds it. I know in that instant her nightmares would recede. She would get better.

I look at the Mum's pale face, struggling with her new English babies, her flat, her battle with the sewage exploding through the manhole in the garden. She has hardly enough money to make her children porridge for supper, tea and breakfast; this is the new Millennium in Sheffield. I ask her about the family she has left behind. Her mother is dead, her sister is dead, she feels cold inside she says, very cold. She worries she cannot love her little girl enough or her babies or the husband. She lies on the sofa, her head on a cushion and closes her eyes.

"What would your mother think?" I ask.

Her mother wanted her to be a nurse; she was good at chemistry at school.

"What would your mother tell you to do now, here?"

"Learn English," she said. She went home and rose from the sofa and went to college. It was February. I made an appointment to see her when the daffodils came and in the springtime everything would be better.

Their asylum papers come through in March. Both parents attend college to study English; the little girl helps them with their homework.

In the summer they return to tell me about their new house and give me yellow and orange flowers.

Chapter 16

2007 - Return to London

There is nothing like returning to a place that remains unchanged to find the ways in which you yourself have altered.
Nelson Mandela

I returned to London, to another CAMHS in a multi-ethnic area. The NHS was changing and another economic crisis looming. Walking through this clinic's doors were women in flowing robes, wearing masks and covered heads, they carried babies on their backs, in buggies, in their arms wrapped in blankets. Families arrived from war-torn African countries, hardly able to speak, families from Portugal, Malta, trying to understand how to organise housing, help their children, and pluck up courage to talk to a teacher. There were children who refused to attend school, children who ate too much, teenagers who ate too little. There were refugees, migrants, non-English speakers. We saw families together, sullen teenagers, little toddlers. We drove across the borough to support families in school meetings, to work alongside social workers, to encourage mothers to take their children into children's centres; we liaised with the police.

I sent emails to my old colleagues:

Today was my first day in my new London CAMHS. They forgot I was coming and weren't sure if there was money to pay me. The kitchen is too small to sit around and chat and NO BISCUITS (gasp, horror, aargh!!)

However a guy appeared on a tricycle with sandwiches and fantastic homemade soup which I needed by 9.30am to revive me after the train journey - Northern Line, Silver Link and the aroma of sweaty armpits.

The lilac files are kept in a special room where I was incarcerated to go through the waiting list and choose half a dozen I would cope with on my own.

After putting to one side the three cases with murdered parents and a boy involved in a major shooting incident, I picked up a couple which needed interpreters. I was unable to work out what language, what form to fill in to request them, or where to fill in the room booking chart.

A severe secretary who said I have to use standard letters for first appointments or do them myself and handover the coffee money.

We have three family therapists, but one has had a heart attack, one is on maternity leave and the third has been off six weeks with stress.

I have been given a swipe card to get in and out of the building which I have already mislaid and daren't tell anyone.

I am attending my fifth training course since employed by the NHS to learn their system for entering data into the computer (gulp again!!)

Its good, though, everyone was very warm and friendly, I'm going to be fine.

WEEK TWO

Just a note to give the next instalment; managed to fill in the wrong week on the room booking chart and as a consequence, had to see my families in the corridor.

I keep running out to the garage next door to buy bars of galaxy, dark chocolate is good for the heart.

Hardly anyone is English. Their issues are so much to do with cultural identity and being immigrants. The kids dream of their homeland......

I return to my work with parents, often single mothers and their babies. I want to resist the despair of poverty, educational and social deprivation, I want to cling to hope and possibility. I pick up a video camera.

Seeing is Believing[7]

> *To video (photograph): it is to put on the same line of sight the head, the eye and the heart.*
> Henri Cartier-Bresson

In the 1970s, I balanced a large video camera between my hands. I filmed mothers and babies, I was intrigued by their pleasure in watching themselves 'on TV', their surprise at seeing themselves managing squirming infants <u>in their laps.</u> Now, still with video, I use a camcorder

7 - In Seeing is Believing parents see their own and their children's strengths, considering their infant's perspective through self-observation. The aim of this time-limited intervention is to strengthen the bond between parents and young children. The edited video becomes the focus of conversation. The skill lies in choosing what to look at and what to discard. Video can capture the unexpressed, lying beyond words, reveals nuances of feeling. The process is repeated; emerging positive stories, witnessed by the therapist, lead the parent to re-story his or her abilities and knowledge of parenting. It provides mothers with concrete evidence that they are doing a good job in order to do more with increased self-confidence. Video work transcends cultural, linguistic and intellectual difficulties. Parents receive a DVD showing their progress at the end of the work.

nestling in my palm whilst filming. Most parents want the best for their babies, although difficult circumstances constantly undermine their confidence in parenting. I film parent and child together, for several minutes. I choose good clips, sometimes very short - the eye contact, the mother's rapt attention, the baby's arms and legs dancing, the toddlers smile. I meet again with the mother: we watch together, enjoying these edited images. This process is repeated several times. This initiative was called 'Seeing is Believing'.

I worked with Sara, a clinical psychologist:

Sara

> "*I have spent much of my qualified working-life looking down the metaphorical black hole of mental illness and trauma. How inspiring to find a method where video frames hold time still. The family and therapist can safely explore the multiple layers of potential that often go unnoticed. I witnessed the potential of the video-clips to unlock parents' self-belief and reflect on their child's inner world so that they could develop a close relationship.*
> *Watching myself on video engendered self-reflection, making links between parent-child and therapist-parent and therapist-child interactions. In supervision, these multiple layers of attachment and interaction could also be frozen in time and examined later.*"

We tell stories about ourselves. They are influenced by stories told to us about our families, ancestors as well as ourselves. Video images connect back to earlier hopeful experiences, reconnect with the treasured parts our lives already led and help us find them again.

Parents' Comments

"Being a parent's not easy you need help, especially away from home"
(Refugee from Iran).

"When I see the first video and the last it is a lot of change, I learn it's not that hard to make them happy"
(A Lithuanian parent).

"He's learning from me, like a mother should teach her children"
(Mother with severe learning disability).

"I watch learn Joseph is just a small child, in a small world and he needs me to be in his small world as well"
(A Polish single mother).

"I saw I was OK with him and get the confidence"
(Eritrean asylum seeker).

'The feedback is really good, you see yourself, you see your child and someone else is re-enforcing the things you are seeing"
(Colombian refugee).

Asylum seeker mothers and their babies

Every gesture we make, the very way we move, our grace or lack of it....reflect both the country and local culture we have grown up in and that our mothers and those close to us have passed on.
Susie Orbach

Themes of hope and despair were constantly threaded through the time spent with asylum seeker mothers and their babies. To stay focused on the babies and not be distracted by Home Office letters and NHS cuts was difficult.

One day we were drawing. They coloured rainbows, some linked to ground on each side, a bridge from then to now, others disjointed and floating in space. These mothers were acknowledging what was behind them and tentatively, through drawing, explored how they could step ahead. We made footprints, printing a baby foot next to the mother's foot was an image of a future dream.

The mothers place the babies on blankets in a circle. The babies are quiet, watching each other being massaged, singing, listening to their mums' laughter. The women are watching each other's babies.

In my hand I hold a symphony of different greens. I have brought bunches of fresh herbs, parsley with frilly edges, soft grey leaves of sage, strong mint from the garden, bright basil smelling of hot sunshine, woody sprigs of tiny-leaved thyme, bluish needles of rosemary. The mothers' heads are bent, inhaling the different odours, laughing, remembering the aromas of cooking in faraway places.

They waft the herbs under the babies noses, they open their eyes and podgy fingers stretch out to clutch the leaves, other uncurl their toes and their noses reach out for more, we sit fascinated, watching.

They share lullabies, listening in different languages. One Googles *lullabies* on her phone, they all do the same and find lullabies in their own languages. One young woman, Libyan with no English, sits quietly. She wears a veil round her head and pyjamas. She removed her hijab when she came into the room, a sign of feeling safe in the all-female environment of women who had undergone similar experiences to her. No need for words. She starts singing. Everyone sits very still to catch her words, the babies are silent, a little turn of the head, a kicking leg, her lullaby is in Arabic. As she sings a tear slowly rolls down her cheek, the Liberian mother next to her puts her hand on her arm, they are by her side.

Not everything has a name. Some things
lead us into the realm beyond words
This is like that small room in the fairy-tales
You glance into it and what you see is not yourself:
For an instance you glimpse the Inaccessible
Where no horse or magic carpet can take you.
And the soul cries out for this.
Alexander Solzhenitsyn

EPILOGUE

So teach us to number our days that we may get a heart of wisdom
Psalm 90:12

Rosh Hashana, Jewish New Year. Jo, a friend, an English rose who has converted to liberal Judaism, has led me to a synagogue. The service is in Hebrew. I listen to the traditional melodies. I watch a woman in a tallit lifting the scroll out of the ark. Three women stand on the bimah, (the podium). Jo is lifting the scroll high above her head. My friend who has chosen to become Jewish. She has studied hard to understand the meaning of the prayers and decipher the dots and squiggles under the Hebrew letters.

I have not chosen. I am here by default, my choice is to turn my back on the scrolls and stay tucked into my safe, secular, English life. Her Shul sets up camp in a church hall. A trestle table is positioned and a portable arc wheeled in, pop-up synagogue.

We are near the end of the service. I watch the black man with a homely Yorkshire accent lift his blue tallit over his head and blow the shofar, to announce the New Year. This moment is many moments, at the end of the service a shofar sounds at one end of the shul then another somewhere else and again and again, until the room is filled with the sound of the rams horn, calling us back many thousand years.

The rabbi calls out and the shofar answers a refrain. One blast is a call, two is an answer and three is the extended sound of suffering. In that fleeting moment I belong to more than the Gornitzky/Weiss family who reached the white cliffs of Dover just in time. It's a call from somewhere else across the desert, the burning sun and the hamsim whipping up sand into my eyes. For a moment I feel like Rachel at the well, I become Miriam, dancing to victory with a tambourine. I am Sara getting old.

After the service we sing a blessing for the wine and the apple and honey to sweeten the coming year, and then perform TASHLICH, a ceremony, which originated in mediaeval Eastern Europe. Forming a small procession, we straggle over to the park in the autumn sunshine, a few children, skipping and jumping, a man still with his tallit wrapped over his shoulders. All the men and couple of the women wear hats, one in a wheel chair and me, my father's bar mitzvah kepi balanced on my head. We are searching for flowing water to cast bread, symbolic of the sins we have committed during the past year. If the water carries the bread away our sins are lifted from our shoulders and we can start anew. This is Stoke Newington and we only find stagnant water with algae, maybe a tiny trickle. We gather close together on the bridge, listening to our sins being chanted by the rabbi.

A group of Muslim women in hijabs pushing buggies wheel their babies closer to watch. An elderly black man drives his electric wheelchair between us, greeting the lady in a wheelchair who is now casting her bread vigorously. Small children on scooters lick ice-creams and are curiously watching us. Two young girls in minute shorts ask for a piece of bread to feed the ducks. A couple of brothers, wearing dreadlocks and yellow tee-shirts, black mirror sunglasses, chew slowly as they stand looking us up and down. A large Polish family sets up a picnic and waves fat pork sausages at us, to eat with our bread.

I am being a Jew in public. I am with my community and participating in an ancient ritual. I am being watched by others, all of different colours, ethnicity, faiths. We are all gathered in the sunshine in Clissold Park. How many of us have fathers from somewhere else? How many of us wonder where home is?

A tall boy appears before me clapping his hands in my face. I'm startled momentarily, then enchanted by his eyes which shine with excitement. We smile at each other and take turns clapping. He changes his rhythm, and we each clap again. Suddenly he turns away and walks down the path clapping to himself over and over. I no longer exist. He'd chosen someone who had once stepped out of an egg, who'd clapped rhythm patterns, in circles, across time. Someone who was about to drive her car through the Channel Tunnel back into Europe, to Eastern France, only an hour from Switzerland, only an hour from Germany.

Alsace, home in the foothills of the Vosges.

Acknowledgements

Thank you to my Mum for the rabbit tail.
Thank you to my Dad for making me listen to music.

**

Remembering with love my brother Johnny Gorney, our whisperings in German, our shared impersonations of the émigrés; his reassuring presence until he was no longer there.

**

Throughout my working life, in Community Arts, in education and as a psychotherapist I have worked alongside many extraordinary, energetic and gifted people. Their compassion and skill always amazed me. I express my deepest gratitude for the projects we completed together.

Thanks especially to:

ED Berman, David Powell, Jon Rust, Paul Malkin, Tony Coult, Carola Chataway, Sara Pearlman, Hugh Fox, Jo Weinberger, Liz Leyh, Sue Roberts , David Stafford, John Perry, Romy Cheeseman,

Also thanks to the inspirational and dedicated clinicians I worked alongside in NHS CAMHS teams in Sheffield and London.

It was a privilege to work with the families who struggled, the women raising their babies and toddlers against the odds and above all the many children who have made me laugh, made me cry and with whom there is always possibility and hope.

**

The book

Massive heartfelt gratitude to those with whom I have collaborated in the creation of this book.

First and foremost my editor the talented Kate Thompson for coaxing, encouraging, gently questioning; for her inexhaustible supply of insightful comments; for her deft hand always ready to adjust the syntax, enormous thanks.

Profound thanks to Claude Dollinger for his limitless curiosity about my family story, his painstaking transcriptions of my parents' letters and his sketches of the Sefton Hotel, Douglas, Isle of Man, without barbed wire.

Thanks to Julie Wheelwright for convincing me there was a story to tell, a book to write and getting me started. Thanks to Mary White, ready to listen to snippets and read early drafts. Thank you to Jo Ryam for leading me to Clissold Park, Anita Franklin for her encouragement and to my cousin Ronnie Gorney, willing to share family stories and help me remember the bits I forgot.

I am grateful to Julia Nelki for her companionship as we researched and explored family history during our visits to the Isle of Man and to Michael Gopfert for conquering volcanic ash. I am indebted to Yvonne Cresswell, curator of social history of the Manx Heritage Museum, Douglas for making herself and the museum resources so generously available and to Huddersfield Local Studies Library for tracing information about my grandfather.

Thanks to Gerald and Anne Goodwin for telling me their own family stories, departure from Germany, arrival in Britain and internment. Thanks to Sabine Schaffner for her comments.

Thanks to Milk and Honey Tours, Berlin, for researching my family and Philip and Sandra Gangloff for the loan of their apartment during our visit.

Much gratitude to David Johnson, Patty Pitman, Rosemary Dighton, Shirley Duff-Gray, Steve Thomas, Rabbi Judith Levitt, Ed Webb-Ingall, who all read an earlier draft . Their comments were profound, sensitive, astute and gave me the confidence to finish.

Above all, thanks to John Knights, my most loved companion, my best friend and faithful listener - whose love, honesty and unshakable belief in my writing has kept me going until there was a book.